Chicago Cooks

45 PERFECT Recipes for the PASSIONATE Palate

Jonathan Horwich & Carol Montag

Illustrations by Francisco Alvarez Rincon

Cover art: *Baseball Girl* by Karl Wirsum, 1964, Chicago, Illinois
Reprinted with the artist's permission.

Printed and bound in the United States of America
Typeset in Franklin Gothic
Designed by Lidia Varesco Design

Printed by Dupli-Group

The information given in the histories of some food items was
compiled from research and is not attributed to any one author,
but rather under the copyleft principle.

In memory of our mothers, Jane S. Jacobs
and Ruth P. Horwich, whose style, impeccable
taste, and support of all the arts, including the
high art of dining, stimulated our vision
and encouraged our effort.

We love you and we miss you everyday.

Table of Contents

Introduction

One cannot think well, love well, sleep well, if one has not dined well.

— VIRGINIA WOOLF, *A ROOM OF ONE'S OWN*

Why buy this cookbook? What do we offer that makes it so special?

Well, have you ever looked at a cookbook with so many recipes that you have no idea which ones are magical or even very good? How do you find and choose truly great recipes? A cookbook can have hundreds of recipes and finding the best, perfect, or the definitive one can take months or years of testing. This was the exact problem we kept running into and it is what inspired us to write this cookbook.

We feel we have solved the problem. We have researched, tested, researched and tested again, and created a book with 45 extraordinary recipes. No more wondering, no more hoping and testing.

We have chosen to write a cookbook with fewer recipes, but ones that we find very close to perfection. We realize that this is a subjective matter and so we have tried to highlight recipes that are so good in their particular genre, that you will be hard pressed to find better ones. As well, we give you some food history, some helpful cooking tips, and some equipment suggestions.

In *Chicago Cooks: 45 Perfect Recipes for the Passionate Palate,* the basics are covered for any kind of meal. Not every food category is included here, but the ones we have chosen represent a foundation any cook will need to provide for a family or to entertain brilliantly.

While neither of us is a professionally trained chef, we have written a book for those new cooks, young cooks, and home cooks who are curious about how to get more professional results or wonder about the detail of how to achieve a finished dish.

As children, we grew up with wonderful food in our homes. We traveled widely with our parents, and were treated to fine dining at great restaurants. However, for us, it has been nearly impossible to find recipes that are as stellar and match those childhood experiences.

We are not just referring to what people think of as gourmet food. The same standard of excellence, the same exacting technique, should also be applied to basic foods as well, such as egg salad, coleslaw, bacon, grilled cheese sandwiches, guacamole, applesauce, and yes, even hard-boiled eggs.

It is our belief that when you use exact and correct cooking techniques, with the best ingredients, you will produce an extraordinary result for any food. Our seared roast beef, for example, is the best piece of beef our testers have tried. Each one of them said it was better than any roast beef they had experienced. The same can be said for our Chicago baby back ribs, potato cakes (made from left over mashed potatoes), or our oatmeal raisin cookies, to name a few. And yes, even our pan-fried toast cooked in olive oil.

One helpful note; this book is rather text heavy and deliberately so. It is because we have taken the time to describe in detail how to do certain cooking techniques.

We suggest that you take these recipes, first follow them exactly as they are written, and then adapt them to make them your own, using them as the foundation to create new recipes from your culinary imagination.

In that spirit, we have added sections at the end of the book that give you ideas of what to do with quick-to-cook foods and leftovers, called Little Gems and Leftovers. And to help with the basics of how to prepare many of these recipes, there is even a section on Techniques and Equipment.

We hope you will trust us and try these recipes so that you can experience food made with care and passion, food that stimulates your palate, and inspires you to share each recipe with those you love.

Carol Montag
Jonathan Horwich

Acknowledgments

We wish to thank the many good people who supported us throughout this endeavor. We owe a debt of gratitude to our many recipe testers and tasters. They sustained and inspired us to persevere and gave us helpful feedback.

A grateful thank you to Karl Wirsum for his immense talent, inspiration, and permission to use *Baseball Girl*, 1964 as our cover art.

The idea for this book came about because of our love of cooking and in particular cooking for Ruth P. Horwich and her many dinner guests. While she is no longer with us, this book expresses the heart and soul of her kitchen and her love of elegant entertaining. No one did it better than Ruth and it was our pleasure to cook for her and her many friends.

BEGINNINGS

The most remarkable thing about my mother is that for 30 years she served the family nothing but leftovers. The original meal has never been found.

— CALVIN TRILLIN

Guacamole

SERVES 1 OR 2

This is hands-down the best guacamole recipe we have ever eaten. And we have eaten a lot of them.

Many guacamole recipes fail in our opinion because they are overly creamy and smooth. The avocado already provides such a texture, so in contrast, we prefer a chunky consistency.

Guacamole should be made with high quality avocados and should be made just before serving. It needs only five minutes or so for the flavors to develop, though you may allow it to sit for as long as 15 minutes. It should not be made hours in advance and refrigerated.

This recipe lends itself beautifully to different palates; some people will increase or decrease the amount of and type of chilies, or amount of onion, or lime juice, or cilantro. First try the portions listed below and then experiment from there.

With these ingredients and with our method of preparing guacamole, you will have a healthy and delicious appetizer, snack, addition to egg dishes, filling for tortillas, or as an accompaniment to your own entrée.

We often serve it with our warm, Homemade Corn Chips (see recipe, page 6) which elevates the guacamole to another plateau.

½ teaspoon garlic, finely minced, or to taste

1 to 2 teaspoons of Serrano pepper or to taste (unseeded, finely chopped)

1 ½ tablespoons white onion, not too finely chopped

¼ teaspoon course salt, or more to taste

1 medium or 2 small Hass avocados (firm, but with some give to them)

2 tablespoons ripe tomatoes, seeded and not too finely diced

1 ½ to 2 teaspoons, lime juice, or to taste, freshly squeezed

1 ½ tablespoons fresh cilantro finely chopped

TOOLS

- Mortar and pestle (or failing that, a suitable bowl)
- Wooden spoon
- Sharp knives

1 Do your *mise en place* as per the ingredient list (see Tip 1) and place in small bowls ready for use: garlic, Serrano pepper, white onion, salt, tomatoes, lime juice, and cilantro.

2 **In the mortar (or suitable bowl), mash garlic, Serrano pepper, onion, and salt together with a pestle or wooden spoon to a liquid-like consistency to release flavor.**

3 **Prepare the avocado by slicing it in two, lengthwise, around the pit with a suitable knife.** Twist the two halves apart by holding one in each hand and twisting to cause the two halves to separate.

4 **Remove the pit by tapping a sharp knife into it, rotating the knife left or right to disengage the pit from the skin, and pulling the pit up and out.** Then discard the pit by scraping the pit against the underside of the rim of the garbage can or other suitable container, to pull it from the knife (see Tip 2).

5 **Hold one half of the avocado at a time and cut ½ inch wide pieces with a small knife across the short side of the avocado. Turn and slice ½ inch pieces across the long side to create a dice.**

6 **Scoop the diced pieces out with a spoon and add them to the mixture in the mortar or bowl.**

7 **Add tomatoes, lime juice, and cilantro. Gently mix with a wooden spoon.** Take care not to mash the avocado too much.

8 **Allow the flavors to marry up for 5 or so minutes, and then serve.** Note: This marry-up time is welcome if you're serving the guacamole with homemade chips (see recipe, page 6) as you can cook the chips and serve them hot or warm as the guacamole develops its flavor.

TIPS

1. *Mise en place* is a French term used by chefs to refer to the preparation of all ingredients before beginning any recipe. Each ingredient is placed in its own prep bowl and assembled on a cutting board or suitable surface. As you follow the recipe directions, each ingredient has already been measured and gathered in one place, making your cooking more accurate and more efficient. If you get in the habit of doing the *mise en place* each time you cook, you will see its advantage.
2. Caution: the pit is very slippery so trying to remove it from the knife with your hand is very dangerous. If you are not comfortable scraping it off the knife on the underside of a garbage can, pull the pit off of the knife wearing an oven glove or thick kitchen cloth or, to begin with, scoop it out with a spoon.
3. Every good chef should own a mortar and pestle. They are invaluable and produce wonderful flavors such as in this recipe where we crush the garlic, onions, pepper and salt to release their inherent flavors. Once you grind or crush peppercorns, salt, garlic, or other spices with a mortar and pestle you'll know why chefs use them for enhanced flavor.

About Guacamole

Guacamole's main ingredient is the avocado, which some think of as a near perfect food. It is biologically classified as a fruit (Carol's grandmother used to call the avocado an alligator pear!) but shares much in common with vegetables. It is very healthy and while quite caloric because of its high fat content, it is exactly the kind of unsaturated fat we need. Its carotenoid antioxidants are concentrated near the dark green part of the avocado's peel.

The avocado's origin is Mexico, documented by archeologists as appearing around 5,000 to 7,000 BC. It was the ancient Aztecs who developed a type of guacamole. The word comes from "ahuacatl" (which means avocado) that became "guaca" and "mole" (which means sauce).

Homemade Corn Chips

SERVES 1 TO 2

We don't know about you, but one of our favorite culinary experiences is "crunch"—whether it is the crunchy skin of our roasted chicken, the crunchy first bite of our grilled cheese sandwich, or our crunchy, cold coleslaw. Nothing has a more satisfying and delicious crunch than homemade, warm, corn tortilla chips.

This is true comfort food.

These are so simple to make, but your guests will think you slaved for hours putting them together.

There are any number of uses for these corn chips; we love them all by themselves, but surely they are a great scoop for dips and salsas, a grand platform for your take on nachos, or as an accompaniment to a salad. These chips lend a savory element crumbled on top of our Sweet Corn Soup (see recipe, page 9) or along side any sandwich. And, of course, they are paired perfectly with our guacamole recipe (see recipe, page 4), providing one of the most delicious culinary marriages we know. You could do no worse at any Super Bowl party just serving these chips with guacamole.

Follow the directions below and see for yourself how easy and tasty these are compared to the store-bought variety.

Vegetable, grapeseed or peanut oil

Corn Tortillas (the best you can find)

Optional: Kosher or Sea Salt

TOOLS

- Cast iron pan or pot, at least 3" high, or a Le Creuset Dutch Oven.
- Large knife (for cutting the corn tortillas)
- Metal spider, tongs or even a slotted metal spoon (to lift the chips in and out of the oil).
- Oil thermometer
- Paper Towels

1 **Pour about ¼ to ½ inch of oil into a large iron skillet or pot.**

2 **Heat the oil in the cast iron skillet or pot until it reaches between 225 and 250 degrees, no hotter.** Too hot and you'll burn the chips, which cook very quickly even at this heat.

3 **Stack 3 to 4 tortillas and cut into four pie-shaped sections.**

4 **When the oil is heated, carefully place several chips into the hot oil in a single layer.** Avoid having chips on top of one another.

5 **Cook briefly until just golden brown. Do not overcook.**

6 **Remove and drain on paper towels.**

7 Optional: Sprinkle lightly with salt if you wish. Serve while still warm with Guacamole (see recipe, page 4), salsa, nachos, or with other foods.

TIPS

1. We prefer using a large knife that easily spans the tortilla cutting it into four equal sections with two slices of the knife. Each cut section will become a corn chip when cooked.
2. Use a spider, tongs or even a slotted metal spoon to move the chips into and out of the oil.
3. Optional: If you wish, flip the chips over once, briefly, while cooking for more even cooking.

Carrot Soup

SERVES 8, ABOUT 2 ½ QUARTS OF SOUP

As soup goes, and we adore it, this soup is truly magical. The secret is nuance of flavor. The addition of small amounts of special ingredients such as wine, ginger, lemon juice, and coconut milk gives it a subtle, yet complex flavor. In fact, when we found that chicken stock overwhelmed the soup, covering up its delicate flavors, we decided to use only one cup of chicken stock to add a bit of its unique flavor and then used a very high quality vegetable stock for the remainder of the liquid.

We also found that the subtle flavor of the soup is greatly enhanced by allowing the finished soup to rest and marry about 48 hours before serving. That may seem like an inordinately long period of time, but patience will yield a subtle flavor that is unsurpassed (see Tip 3). The result is a world-class, delicious soup.

Serve it warm, garnished with a swirl of crème fraîche, a sprinkling of chives or dill, several croutons, or a slice of Pan-Fried Toast on the side if you prefer (see recipe, page 56).

If you wish to take it over the top, serve with chunks of good quality shrimp, crabmeat, or lobster. Divine.

We have had great success serving it at dinner parties and we think you will, too. Its gorgeous color heralds the introduction to a great meal.

3 pounds carrots

¼ cup grapeseed oil

1 tablespoon minced garlic

2 tablespoons minced fresh ginger

2 tablespoons minced green onion (scallions)

Pinch of red pepper flakes

2 tablespoons honey or to taste

1 tablespoon salt or to taste

½ teaspoon freshly ground white pepper

½ teaspoon turmeric

1 cup chicken stock

7 cups vegetable stock. We use Savory Choice Vegetable Broth. (Too much chicken or meat stock provides too strong a flavor)

1 cup heavy cream

¼ pound (1 stick) unsalted butter

1 tablespoon lemon juice

1 tablespoon white wine

1 tablespoon coconut milk

TOOLS

- Vegetable peeler
- Large chef's knife
- Large soup pot
- Professional blender such as the Vitamix
- Large bowl
- Glass storage jars
- Wooden (or silicone) paddle or spoon
- Optional: Food processor to slice the carrots thinly and consistently

1 **Peel carrots and slice them very thin.** We found the thinner, the more flavor is imparted to the soup. We often use a food processor with a cutting blade that results in consistently thin carrot slices about half the thickness of a quarter. They are so thin they are flexible to the touch.

2 **In a large soup pot, heat the oil over medium heat.**

3 **Add the garlic, minced ginger, green onions, pepper flakes and sauté stirring continuously until they are aromatic and glossy but have not yet begun to brown, about 2 to 4 minutes.**

4 **Add the carrots, honey, salt, pepper, and turmeric. Cook 5 to 10 minutes more, stirring and folding constantly so the flavors develop from the sautéing.**

5 **Add the vegetable and chicken stock, heat to a simmer and cook until the carrots are just tender.** This will take about 15 to 20 minutes if the carrots are sliced thin and about 30 or more minutes if carrots are thicker. Do not overcook the carrots or they will lose their flavor (see Tip 2).

Carrot Soup *continued*

6 **Once cooled down, transfer the soup in batches to a blender, adding some of the butter with each blending so all of the butter is used. In one of the batches add the tablespoon of coconut milk so it blends in well. Blend the mixture in batches for at least 45 seconds to a minute.** Use a Vitamix or comparable blender taking care not to overfill the blender as the high speed spinning motion will send the hot soup out of the top. Fill the container ⅓ to ½ full.

7 **Transfer each batch to a large bowl or container capable of holding all the soup.** Allow the blended soup to cool down a bit in the large bowl.

8 **Add the cream, lemon juice, and wine, stirring them in with a big wooden paddle or spoon.**

9 **Put the soup in glass Mason jars filling them right to the top and let cool uncovered.**

10 **When cool, cover tightly and store in the refrigerator for 48 hours before serving.** It needs this amount of time for the flavors to marry up.

11 **Before serving, adjust the seasoning, especially the amount of salt as cold dissipates saltiness.** If you need or wish to add more salt, pepper, honey, or lemon juice, do so cautiously as more than a small amount can easily overwhelm the delicate flavor of the soup.

To serve, reheat and, optionally, garnish with croutons, crème fraîche, or serve with a slice of Pan-Fried Toast (see recipe, page 56). Or to take it over the top, serve with chunks of good quality shrimp, crabmeat, or lobster.

TIPS

1. Only use a professional blender, such as the Vitamix, which creates a very smooth consistency if left on high for some 45 seconds a batch. Take care to not overfill the blender as the high-speed spinning motion will send the hot soup out of the top of the container. Fill the container ⅓ to ½ full.
2. Avoid the common error of overcooking soup. Simmer it just enough to soften the carrots so they do not become mushy. In the last five minutes of cooking turn off the flame to prevent the soup from overcooking and allow the soup to cool down. Err on the side of undercooking.
3. The advantage of preparing the soup 48 hours in advance is that it not only marries the flavors, but it allows the cook to prepare ahead and merely heat up the soup at serving time.

Sweet Corn Soup

SERVES 6 TO 8

Of all the recipes in this book, this was the most challenging; not because it is difficult, it is not. Not because it has so many steps and so many ingredients, it does not. It is because we wanted to create a different corn soup, one of subtlety and refinement, yet one that had a distinct corn flavor. And that was not easy.

After much testing, experimenting, and refining, we have created what we believe is a delicious-tasting corn soup.

With the summer flavors of real sweet corn, the infusion of fresh thyme, the additions of cream, cognac, and some heat from red pepper flakes, this soup is full of delicate, nuanced, yet complex corn flavor. It is a wonderful addition to any meal.

Served with shrimp or lump crab the soup is absolutely irresistible.

Warning: More so than most soups and as we direct you in our carrot soup recipe, this recipe does not taste right for 48 hours. So prepare ahead. And when the time comes, it is easy to serve, just heat it up.

TOOLS

- Stockpot- 8 or more quarts (for making the corn stock)
- Chef's knife
- Strainer
- Large soup pot, 8 or more quarts (for making the soup itself)
- Flat grater with large, ¼" holes (box grater holes are normally not big enough) See illustration on page 11
- Optional: Silicone baking mat (such as Sil Pat) or parchment paper
- Roasting Pan or Wooden Bowl
- Vitamix or other comparable, professional blender
- Large bowl
- 3 to 4 one-quart Mason jars

Ingredients for the stock

5 whole sweet corn cobs, kernels removed and saved for later

Note, to save time you will scrape all 10 cobs of corn at this time and set aside all the kernels for making the soup itself later. Five of those scraped cobs will be used in the stock with the rest of the cobs discarded (See recipe steps and Tip 1)

1 medium yellow onion, roughly cut up in small chunks or slices

Several whole sprigs of fresh thyme

4 cups of water

3 cups vegetable broth (we use a boxed broth made up of individual packets of vegetable broth concentrate called Savory Choice)

Directions for the stock

This stock can be made hours or even days in advance of making the remainder of the soup.

1 **With a large-holed flat grater** (see illustration), **scrape the corn from 10 cobs into a bowl.** This takes about 10 minutes and is worth the extra effort involved, (for the exact method, see Tip 1).

2 **Set the corn and its juice aside in a storage container, glass jar, or bag in the refrigerator for use later in making the soup itself.**

3 **Place 5 of the whole scraped cobs, onion, thyme, and water in a stockpot.** Discard the other 5 cobs. The water will not fully cover the cobs.

4 **Barely simmer for about one hour, stirring occasionally and flipping the corn as needed so all sides cook under the water. Partially cover the pot as the corn simmers, helping to keep in the moisture.**

5 **Discard the cobs from the stock and strain the remainder of the liquid into a bowl.**

6 **Add three cups of vegetable broth, allow to cool down.**

7 **Pour into glass jar(s) and reserve in refrigerator if not making the soup right away.**

Sweet Corn Soup *continued*

Ingredients for the soup

4 tablespoons butter

2 small or medium cloves of garlic, minced

1 medium onion, diced

1 large leek, washed and sliced, white part only

⅛ to ¼ teaspoon red pepper flakes, depending on taste. If you want the soup to have a definite kick, use ¼ to ½ teaspoon.

1 large carrot, peeled and diced

1 large stalk of celery, diced

Corn kernels and juice from 10 ears of fresh sweet corn, scraped as above

2 tablespoons salt

1 cup dry white wine

Corn stock (previously prepared)

Optional: 2 tablespoons coconut milk

6 tablespoons of good quality cognac

1 tablespoon fresh lemon juice

1 cup of heavy cream

Directions for the soup

1 **Prepare all vegetables per the directions under ingredients.** If the stock was prepared earlier take it out of the refrigerator. This is your *mise en place*, as the French say, meaning everything is prepared and ready to go before the actual cooking. This makes life much easier and your cooking more accurate.

2 **Melt butter in the large soup pot.**

3 **Add minced garlic, onions, leeks, and sauté until aromatic. Then add the red pepper flakes sautéing them with the garlic, onions and leeks for a few more minutes.**

4 **Add all the remaining vegetables, salt, and sauté for another few minutes, barely softening the carrots and celery.**

5 **Add the reserved corn (and its juice) from the 10 cobs. Sauté gently for 5 to 8 minutes.**

6 **Add the cup of wine and allow it to cook for several minutes to burn off some of the alcohol.**

7 **Add the corn/vegetable stock you previously made and simmer very gently for 15 minutes, stirring every so often.** In the last 5 minutes, turn off the flame to allow the soup to cool down. Avoid the common mistake of over-cooking as the corn and vegetables will become mushy and lose their fresh flavor. Err on the side of undercooking.

8 **Once cooled down, blend soup mixture in batches for at least 45 seconds to a minute.** Use a Vitamix or comparable blender, taking care not to overfill the blender as the high speed spinning motion will send the hot soup out of the top. Fill the container ⅓ to ½ full.

Optionally, add 2 tablespoons of coconut milk in one of the batches and completely integrate the milk.

9 **Place each blended batch in one large bowl.**

10 **When the soup has cooled to room temperature add 6 tablespoons cognac, 1 tablespoon fresh lemon juice, and finally the cup of heavy cream. Stir thoroughly.**

11 **Pour into large glass jars, store in a refrigerator 36 to 48 hours.** The soup will not develop its correct flavor otherwise (See Tip 2).

12 **When ready to serve, heat up the soup and correct the seasoning as required.**

Optional: Serve with shrimp or lump crabmeat slightly heated and then placed in the hot soup. Or simply serve with Pan-Fried Toast (see recipe, page 56).

TIPS

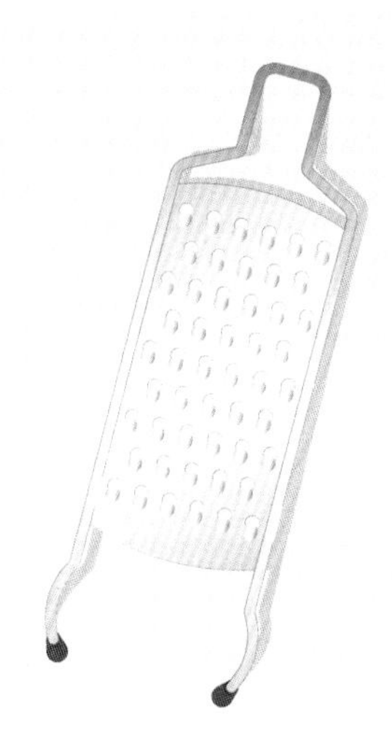

1. We found the best way to strip corn off the cob for this soup is using a flat grater with holes at least ¼" in size, creating a corn that is mushy and wet with corn milk. This adds flavor to the soup. Most box graters don't have ¼" sized holes and do not work for this purpose. If you don't have a large, flat grater with ¼" holes, just slice the corn off the cob with a knife, running close to the cob to get all the juice and corn you can. If using a grater, hold each of the cobs over a roasting pan lined with a silicone baking mat or parchment paper, or just use a giant wooden bowl. Placing the flat grater on a slant with one end on the roasting pan for stability, scrape the corn from each of the 10 cobs. The roasting pan or large wooden bowl will catch all of the kernels as well as the juice from the corn. Carefully hold both sides of the silicone baking mat or sides of a large wooden bowl and remove the scraped corn and its juice to a container or a zip lock bag, reserving it in the refrigerator for the soup. (Often, we first pour the corn from the roasting pan or wooden bowl into a giant measuring cup which has a pour spout making it easy to transfer to bags or containers for storage.)
2. Let soups marry up. This takes time. In the case of the corn soup it takes a good 36 to 48 hours in sealed glass jars to reach a magical flavor. Learn to plan ahead and allow for this. It will result in a very convenient meal as once the flavors have developed, you can serve the soup easily by just heating it up. This also allows you to do the work of making the soup or any recipe at a convenient time, several days ahead and avoiding much of the work involved just before serving the meal.

Vichyssoise

SERVING SIZE, ONE CUP | SERVES AS MANY AS 10

In our entire life we have each had only one great bowl of vichyssoise—Jonathan, at the Palace Hotel in St. Moritz, Switzerland in the early 1970s and Carol, at the Ritz Hotel in Paris in the late 1960s. That was it.

Hence, for this cookbook, we spent months trying to equal or surpass that remembered taste. The secret to our version of Vichyssoise is a subtle flavor, provided here by chives, and small amounts of wine, lemon juice and crème fraîche. After all the experimentation with these flavors, we have come up with a recipe that is the best we have tasted and which retains the original elegance of this soup.

4 leeks, sliced, white parts only, carefully washed

1 medium onion, thinly sliced

4 tablespoons butter

1 teaspoon pepper

2 tablespoons salt

5 potatoes, Idaho or Russets, washed, peeled, thinly and evenly sliced (so they cook faster and consistently)

4 cups vegetable stock (homemade if possible) or we use Savory Choice Vegetable Broth

1 cup chicken stock (homemade if possible)

3 cups whole milk

1 cup cream

1 cup crème fraîche

1 bunch of chives 6 to 8 inches long and 1 to 1 ½ inches in diameter. (At least 6 tablespoons worth)

3 tablespoons lemon juice

3 tablespoons dry white wine

Optional: Chopped chives for garnish

TOOLS

- Chef's knife
- Medium to large sized bowl for soaking potatoes
- Soup pot, 5 to 6 quart size
- Large measuring cup
- Blender, such as a Vitamix
- Large bowl for receiving blended soup
- Glass jars with lids for storing

1 **Wash and peel the potatoes. Slice them thinly and of a consistent thickness.** Set aside in a large bowl of cold water so they do not discolor.

2 **In a large, deep pot, sauté the leeks, onions, salt, and pepper in the butter until soft and slightly brown.**

3 **Add the thinly sliced potatoes and stir to distribute and cook about 5 to 10 minutes, stirring often.** This will develop potato flavor.

4 **Add the vegetable and chicken stock and bring to a simmer, stirring occasionally, for about 15 to 25 minutes.** When the potatoes just yield to a knife point or fork, they are done. Do not overcook or the soup will lose flavor. Let the mixture cool in the pot, but know it will continue cooking while cooling down (referred to as carry-over cooking). Account for this in judging doneness.

5 **Once the mixture is no longer hot, purée small batches of the soup for about 45 seconds in the blender until very, very smooth** (see Tips 1 and 2). Put the puréed soup in a large bowl as you proceed.

6 **Let the mixture cool down in preparation for the addition of milk and cream.** (If added while the soup is hot, the cream and milk could curdle and the soup will contain small pebbles of the dairy instead of the velvet-like texture you are trying to achieve.)

7 **Stir in the milk and cream into the large bowl of soup.**

8 **From the large bowl, purée one batch again in the blender** (about ½ way up the blender jar) **with the chives and the crème fraiche until no chive pieces are visible.**

9 **Pour the batch back into the large bowl with the rest of the soup, add the wine and lemon juice, and stir in completely.** Let cool further. You can prevent a skin forming by laying parchment paper on the surface. Or better yet, just stir it every so often as it cools down.

When at room temperature, store in clean glass jars, allowing the flavors to marry at least overnight. We have found the soup only fully marries up and tastes right after 24-48 hours.

10 Taste the soup the next day and correct seasoning, adding more salt, pepper and if desired, more fresh lemon juice and white wine, both in very small amounts to maintain the delicacy of the soup and the subtlety of flavor. Chill thoroughly (preferably another full day) and serve cold or near room temperature with chopped chives as a garnish as desired.

TIPS

1. Fill the blender jar about ⅓ to ½ full. Otherwise the soup might overflow the container and cause a mess. Also it is easier for the blender to do its job with it ½ full or ⅓ full.
2. Use a professional blender when blending soup. Most home blenders do not do a truly complete job of blending ingredients to a velvet smooth consistency. So use a powerful blender like the Vitamix which makes a very, very smooth soup. And of course, pour the soup into a large bowl as you progress. Take care not to overfill the blender as the high-speed spinning motion will send the hot soup out of the top. Fill the container ⅓ to ½ full.
3. This soup is delicious served hot as well as cold. Heat over low or at the most, medium heat, preferably with a diffuser or double boiler, until the desired temperature is reached. Too much heat could cause the soup to break or curdle.

About Vichyssoise

Vichyssoise is pronounced *vishy swaz* after Vichy, the birthplace of its creator and *ssoise*, the French suffix meaning belonging to or related to.

We think of Vichyssoise as a classic summer soup and as a true French treat. However, that is only partially true. The chef who invented it was indeed French, Louis Diat. But, in 1917, he found himself transported to the Ritz Carlton in Manhattan where he reinvented his mother's leek and potato soup. It was such a success, that guests insisted that it be served year round, not just in the summer months where it was presented in a shallow soup cup tucked into a bed of shaved ice.

Chilled Cucumber-Yogurt Soup

SERVES 2 TO 4

This singular and unusual tasting soup has tangy yogurt as its foundation in combination with cucumbers, fresh dill, and the kick of garlic. The ingredients combine to make a delicious, quick, summer soup and there is no cooking involved. Thickened with yogurt in place of cream, it may remind some of tzaziki, the Greek yogurt sauce, but it is less herb-filled.

A gorgeous pale green when completed, the soup is made in a blender, and is a highly flavorful addition to your warm weather menu. When you feel like a light meal without heating up your kitchen, serve this with our Pan-Fried Toast (see recipe, page 56) or a crusty French bread. You need nothing else to satisfy your spring or summer palate.

3 cucumbers, peeled and seeded, and quartered

2 tablespoons olive oil

3 cups yogurt (we use 2% Greek yogurt)

Fresh dill (a cluster of sprigs about 1 ½ to 2 inches in diameter by about 6 inches long, woody ends trimmed)

1 clove of garlic, peeled

1 tablespoon white vinegar

1 tablespoon salt

½ teaspoon white or black pepper

TOOLS

- Vegetable peeler
- Blender (professional grade, like the Vitamix)
- Glass jar or large glass bowl

1 **Into the blender first put the cucumbers, olive oil, yogurt, followed by the dill, garlic cloves, vinegar, salt and pepper.** While the machine is off, push the ingredients down so they are somewhat in contact with the blades.

2 **Blend until very smooth and with all ingredients incorporated completely.** It should be pale green in color with no particles visible in it. About 45 to 60 seconds.

3 **Pour into glass jars and chill at least 24 hours or more.** The flavors need time to marry up and integrate, more so than most recipes. Do not serve immediately as the soup may be too sharp or strong tasting.

4 **After 24 hours or more (but not less), taste and correct seasoning,** including salt, pepper, garlic, and vinegar. We find we rarely need to adjust anything but a little salt or pepper.

Optional: Serve with a garnish of crème fraîche or sour cream sprinkled with chopped dill. We normally accompany ours with Pan-Fried Toast (see recipe, page 56).

TIPS

In filling any blender always put the most liquid and soft ingredients in first. If you do not do this, the blades will just spin with the solid food resting above the blades. If this occurs, you will have to use a plunger of some kind to push the ingredients into the blade. The Vitamix has a dedicated plunger system that allows you to do this while the machine is still running, as the plunger cannot hit the blades. Other blenders may not be safe in this regard, so exercise caution, and turn off the machine before pushing the ingredients down into the blades.

LIGHT FARE

How can you govern a country that has 246 varieties of cheese?

— CHARLES DE GAULLE

Peewee Pizza

SERVING SIZE: 1 TORTILLA PER PERSON

We actually don't like pizza. This is particularly strange as we are from Chicago where deep dish pizza reigns supreme. Jonathan invented this healthier, lighter alternative as an easy-to-eat snack or as a quick delicious meal. We believe it is more delicate and better tasting than standard pizza. The secret is to use a light touch of the freshest ingredients and superb cheeses along with corn tortillas instead of the traditional, but heavier dough.

We cook Peewee Pizzas on the stovetop in either a carbon steel pan like the de Buyer, a stainless steel All-Clad pan, a cast iron Lodge skillet, or more often, the round 14-inch cast iron baking (pizza) pan by Lodge.

Because we like a thin, crisp crust we use a metal or iron pan with a little olive oil to prevent sticking and to form a crust. And we push the heat up to make the corn tortillas nearly taste like corn chips.

Use these ingredients as a basic starting point and vary or add to these as you wish. For instance, we love greens on the pizzas such as arugula, or fresh spinach often topped with a fried egg, and sometimes even with bacon crumbled or cut into strips. We often add slices of avocados and a dollop of sour cream.

These pizzas serve as a quick, convenient, and delicious meal or appetizer anytime. When we don't feel like preparing an elaborate meal, but want something special, we often turn to Peewee Pizzas.

1 corn tortilla per person (normally about 5 to 6 inches in diameter. Get the best quality tortillas you can)

Gruyère cheese, shredded

Optional: goat or other creamy cheese

4 to 5 black or green olives pitted and sliced in half or fourths

2 to 3 tablespoons red, green and yellow bell peppers (or just one or two of the varieties) seeded and diced, but not finely

1 to 2 tablespoons olive oil

Optional:

Red onion diced, sparingly used

Thinly sliced sun-dried or roasted tomatoes

Arugula, cilantro or baby spinach

Sautéed mushrooms

Thinly sliced avocado

A dollop of sour cream

TOOLS

- Cheese grater
- Long sharp knife
- Skillet – carbon steel pan, iron skillet, stainless pan or the Lodge 14-inch round cast iron baking pan
- Spatula

1 **Lay the corn tortilla on a cutting board or other flat surface.**

2 **Spread a thin to medium layer of shredded Gruyère cheese to cover the tortilla.** As desired, add more of a creamy cheese, such as a goat cheese for contrast in taste.

3 **Evenly distribute the remaining vegetables (such as diced bell peppers and olives) over the cheese.** Add a small amount of chopped onion if desired or even some arugula on top for a healthy alternative.

4 **Heat one to two tablespoons of olive oil** (enough so the tortilla won't stick to the bottom of the pan) **in a skillet or on a 14-inch round Lodge Baking Pan at medium to medium-high heat.**

5 **When the pan and the oil are just hot, put the pizza in the pan.** Cook by adjusting the flame as needed (we find medium to medium high heat does the trick) so the layer of cheese has time to melt before the bottom of the tortilla burns. You want a crisp tortilla with the cheese just melted, leaving the peppers and olives barely cooked.

6 **Remove to a cutting board and wait about 10 seconds before cutting into quarters with a large, long knife.**

Serve for lunch or as a dinner appetizer.

OPTIONAL

Fry or steam an egg or two and serve over the Peewee Pizza for a divine variation.

For added flavor and variety, we often spread a thin layer of a good artisanal ketchup, such as Stonewall Kitchens Country Ketchup, as a base for the pizza. Followed by a sprinkling of cheeses and veggies and a fried egg, this addition adds color as well as tang to the pizza.

TIPS

1. The cheese is shredded so it melts easily. Get a very good Gruyère as the main base, and as desired, mix in a little high quality goat cheese, or other creamy cheese to taste. *Both these cheeses should be a basic food in your refrigerator to create various preparations at a moments notice.*
2. Experiment with different toppings including cheeses, eggs (as above) which transform the pizza into another taste experience, spinach, onions, cilantro, fresh or sun-dried tomatoes, peppers to add heat, sautéed mushrooms, or avocado. The variations are endless.

Grilled Cheese

SERVES ONE SANDWICH PER PERSON

This traditional and much-loved comfort food can be elevated to true gourmet status by exacting technique (yes, even a "simple" grilled cheese sandwich needs precise control and method) as well as superb ingredients. In fact, we use these sandwiches, cut into bite-sized pieces, as hors d'oeuvres at dinner parties and they are always devoured.

Do not skimp on the quality of the ingredients including butter, tomatoes, pickles and particularly the bread and cheese. Without superb cheese and bread, the sandwich becomes mundane or at best only good.

2 slices excellent bread per sandwich, such as a fine artisan Italian loaf

Gruyère cheese, shredded. Get the best quality you can find (we shred it while still cold and firm)

A second cheese may be added sparingly, to taste, such as a good quality (soft) goat cheese

The best small or larger artisan tomatoes available, sliced thin (and seeded if desired)

Sweet pickles (we use sweet Wickles Pickles or Bread and Butter pickle chips)

Optional: Crispy cooked bacon (see recipe, page 61)

Unsalted butter

Olive oil (in addition to butter to prevent it from burning)

TOOLS

- Cheese grater
- A large skillet (We found any high quality metal pan works well in creating a nice crust, such as a steel mineral pan by de Buyer, a cast iron skillet, the round flat 14-inch iron baking pan by Lodge, or a stainless steel All-Clad skillet
- Metal spatula

1 **Place bread slices on the cutting board. Cover one side of each sandwich with the following ingredients, in the following order, especially with the cheese on the bottom.**

A. One layer of shredded Gruyère cheese. Optionally you can add a second cheese such as goat, which is always sprinkled to taste. Shred the Gruyère cheese or in the case of crumbly cheeses such as goat, break it up into small pieces, as you want the cheese to melt evenly and quickly.

B. Two slices of thinly sliced tomatoes spread evenly over the cheese.

C. Two to three pickles as desired, spread evenly.

D. Optional: Bacon. Put the cooked and still warm, crisp bacon on top of all the other ingredients.

2 **Place the second slice of bread over all the ingredients and press down to compact the sandwich a bit.**

3 **Meanwhile, in the frying pan, heat enough butter and a little olive oil, on a medium to medium-high flame to barely cover the bottom of the pan** (see Tips 2 and 3).

4 **When the butter and olive oil are hot and melted, but not browned, add the sandwich to the pan.**

5 **Cook the sandwich on medium, to medium high heat in order to allow the cheeses to melt before the bread gets too dark.**

6 **When browned on the first side, turn the sandwich over with a spatula.** You want a crisp exterior that contrasts with the soft, melted interior. (Optional and recommended: if you have the time, turn the sandwich more frequently eventually achieving a crisp exterior on both sides and more evenly heating the sandwich by such frequent turning.)

7 **When the second side is brown and crunchy, turn the sandwich back over to the first side briefly, just before removing from the skillet.** This assures that both sides are warm or hot.

8 **Move each sandwich to a cutting board and using a good quality serrated (bread) knife, carefully slice (use a short fast, but light sawing action) the sandwich into two, three, or four pieces.** Do not press down too hard with the knife or the sandwich will pull apart.

Serve warm, not so hot as to burn your mouth, but never let the cheese get cool before eating.

SERVING SUGGESTION

Serve as the main meal at lunch with high quality potato chips, to accompany soup, or carefully cut up in strips and serve as delicious hors d'oeuvres.

TIPS

1. For a different taste, we sometimes use Ezekial's Low Sodium, Wheat Sprouted Bread (we buy it frozen, and keep it on hand in the freezer, ready to be used whenever needed), lending a completely different texture and flavor than a fine artisan bread.
2. Err on the side of too low a flame, as you want the cheese to melt slowly and consistently. From time to time, press down on each sandwich with a spatula to help the melting process and secure the ingredients. You can always turn up the flame to darken the bread once the cheese is nearly melted.
3. This is not like steak or hamburger where you want a high, immediate sear of the food on contact. With grilled cheese sandwiches the trick is to apply just enough heat to crisp the bread, but not burn it while melting the cheese. If the heat is too high and the sandwich is cooking too quickly, take the pan on and off the burner from time to time to slow cooking as needed.
4. Use a large pan or round, flat, 14-inch Lodge Baking Pan to give yourself room to manoeuver and flip the sandwiches. Do not crowd them together.

Chicken Salad

SERVES 4

We love chicken salad and often use the cold, leftover chicken from our roasted chicken. However, any cold, cooked chicken, be it poached, broiled, baked, or roasted will be greatly enhanced with this version of chicken salad. While it is a great use of leftovers, we often roast a chicken with this salad in mind.

One of America's great cold, summer salads, along with tuna, potato, and egg salad, we find this one especially aromatic because of the herbs and spices added to the chopped, dressed chicken. If you use our recipe for roasted chicken, the leftover chicken will be infused with the herbs used in roasting and the meat will be even more fragrant. The addition of lemon zest added to the mayonnaise gives this salad a fresh and unusual flavor.

The usual caution applies to all of our recipes containing mayonnaise; use it sparingly even if you love it as we do. Your final result will have a more nuanced, subtle flavor, an elegant texture, and the chicken flavor will shine through. You can always add more if it is too dry for your taste. Here, less is more, truly applies.

4 cups roasted, poached, broiled, baked, or other leftover chicken, chopped into bite-sized pieces, skin removed

6 tablespoons or a generous ¼ cup of Hellman's mayonnaise or to taste

1 teaspoon Kosher salt

¼ teaspoon black pepper

1 tablespoon parsley

1 tablespoon fresh tarragon, or to taste, finely chopped

2 tablespoons red onion, chopped, not too finely

2 tablespoons celery, chopped, not too finely

½ teaspoon grated lemon zest

1 tablespoon Dijon mustard

1 tablespoon red wine vinegar

TOOLS

- 1 Large bowl
- 1 Medium bowl
- Chef's knife
- Large spoon or spatula
- Large glass jars with lids

1 **Chop the cold chicken into bite-sized pieces and set aside in the large mixing bowl.**

2 **In the smaller bowl, combine the mayonnaise with the remaining 9 ingredients and mix well.** Err on the side of too little mayonnaise as we advise you above.

3 **Pour the dressing over the chicken, blend it all together with a spatula or wooden spoon.**

4 **Once mixed, store in clean, glass containers with tight lids overnight to allow the flavors to develop.**

5 **Before serving, bring chicken salad almost to room temperature, mixing it well to be sure that the dressing has not separated. Correct seasoning with salt, pepper, and mayonnaise.**

SERVING SUGGESTION

Serve over greens, with tomatoes, cucumbers, and avocado slices or in a sandwich on good artisan bread or on our Pan-Fried Toast (see recipe, page 56).

The David Eyre Pancake—1966

SERVES 4

This is a true classic. In fact, although this recipe fits the overall purpose of this book, it has nothing to do with either one of us or with Chicago. This '60's classic breakfast/brunch recipe is so delicious and dramatic looking when ready to be served, we included it in our book to preserve it in print.

With minor variations, it did appear in a 10 April, 1966 New York Times article by Craig Claiborne who said that David Eyre (then editor of *Honolulu Magazine*) obtained it from a 1919 cookbook entitled *Hotel St. Francis Cookbook,* by Victor Hirtzler. In 2007 it appeared again in a New York Times Magazine article by Amanda Hesser, and in her cookbook, *the Essential New York Times Cookbook.* As time goes forward, we were afraid of losing sight of the recipe, and hence its inclusion here.

We have made no contribution to this recipe. The original recipe from the *Hotel St. Francis Cookbook* (fully included at the end of the text below) has a teaspoon of sugar as part of the egg and flour mixture which was later taken out in the New York Times. We left it in.

The recipe works flawlessly as written. It is a superb pancake that can be served by itself or with eggs, bacon or even as a "breakfast for dinner" dish.

2 eggs

½ cup flour

½ cup milk

Pinch of ground nutmeg

1 teaspoon of sugar

4 tablespoons (½ stick) unsalted butter

2 tablespoons confectioners' sugar

Juice of ½ lemon

Optional: Fig or blackberry jam, pear butter, or any kind of marmalade, for serving

TOOLS

- Mixing bowl
- 12-inch cast iron skillet (no other).
- Fine meshed sieve

1 **Preheat the oven to 425 degrees.**

2 **In a mixing bowl, lightly beat the eggs.**

3 **Add the flour, milk, nutmeg and sugar. Lightly beat until blended but still slightly lumpy.**

4 **On the stovetop, melt the butter in a 12-inch cast iron skillet over medium-high heat.** Be sure and have the butter run all over the inside of the pan so the pancake will not stick to the bottom or sides when it rises.

5 **When the butter is very hot, but not brown, pour in the batter.**

6 **Bake in the oven until the pancake is billowing on the edges and golden brown, about 15 minutes** (see Tip 1).

7 **Working quickly, remove the pan from the oven and, using a fine-meshed sieve, sprinkle the top with the sugar.**

8 **Return to the oven for 1 to 2 minutes more.**

9 **Remove from oven, sprinkle with lemon juice.**

Optionally, serve with jam, pear butter, or marmalade.

The David Eyre Pancake—1966 *continued*

TIPS

The pancake will puff up in the oven, but as it cools when being served, it will fall and become thin.

About The David Eyre Pancake—1966

The original recipe from the cookbook, *Hotel St. Francis Cookbook,* by Victor Hirtzler was written verbatim as follows:

> Two eggs, one-half cup of milk, one-half cup of flour, a pinch of salt, a little nutmeg and one teaspoonful of sugar. Mix well. Have a large frying pan ready with hot butter. Be sure and have the butter run all over the inside of the pan so the pancake will not stick to the sides when it rises. Pour in the batter and place in oven. When nearly done, powder with sugar and put back in oven to brown. Serve with lemon and powdered sugar.

POULTRY

The chicken does not exist only in order to produce another egg. He may also exist to amuse himself, to praise God, and even to suggest ideas to a French dramatist.

— G.K. CHESTERTON, WHAT'S WRONG WITH THE WORLD

Roast Chicken I

SERVES 4 TO 6

There is no meal more comforting than a deliciously roasted chicken with crisp, bronze skin. But how many truly memorable ones have you eaten? Not many, we would bet. Hence, you can understand our obsession for an exact cooking method that produces divine results.

Roast chicken is the staple of every good French cook. In the words of Julia Child, "You can always judge the quality of a cook or restaurant by its roast chicken."

After much trial and error we found two effective techniques, both require an essential pre-salting and not just for a few hours, but for days. Do not let this first step put you off. It takes but a few minutes to fully salt the bird and stick it in the refrigerator out of the way. Actually, it is good planning because after three or four days, at your convenience, you have a meal on hand, ready to cook.

It should be noted that the salting does not make the chicken meat taste salty, although sometimes the skin itself will retain a salty, but delicious flavor.

While the whole purpose of this cookbook is to provide you with what we consider to be a stellar recipe for any given dish, we couldn't resist giving you two variations for roast chicken. Both are delicious, with the first taking longer to cook; the second one requires more physical involvement, but it takes only an hour to cook and is so delicious we present it here as an option. It requires a somewhat smaller chicken and it has no herbs coating the skin, as the first recipe does, because they would burn under high heat. Still, with these differences, the result is beautiful, delicious, and meets all of the requirements of a truly great cook.

The beauty of the first chicken recipe is that you can leave your kitchen without worry, return after two hours to the delicious buttery aroma of chicken roasting with garlic, lemon, and herbs, baste it, and then return to other activities for another hour. The result is so marvelous; the potatoes are fragrant, crisp on the outside, soft and creamy inside, the chicken fall-off-the-bone tender, and the skin crisp and bronzed. Serve with the pan juices over the chicken and potatoes and a vegetable if you must.

We have not experienced better tasting chickens than the two we present to you here.

One 4 to 5 pound chicken

Salt

Fresh herbs; we like thyme, tarragon, marjoram, and rosemary, but use herbs of your choice.

Red Pepper Flakes

Fennel Seeds

Olive oil

1 small lemon, cut in half

1 head of garlic, the top cut off to expose the inner cloves, or if you prefer, separate the cloves, peel them, and crush them slightly.

3 Idaho or Russet potatoes, peeled and cut into several thick slices

Salt and pepper

TOOLS

- A shallow sheet pan to refrigerate salted chicken
- A heavy-duty 12-inch Lodge cast iron skillet, shallow roasting pan, or sheet pan that will hold the chicken and potatoes comfortably
- Long-handled spoon for basting

1 **Remove all innards from the chicken and discard.**

2 **Rinse chicken thoroughly, inside and out, pat very dry with paper towels.**

3 **Salt chicken all over, using about ¾ teaspoon for each pound of chicken.** Coat thoroughly and evenly over the entire chicken.

4 **Wrap the chicken loosely first with parchment paper and then loosely with a second wrapping of foil.** Although the parchment is optional, we prefer it against the skin of the bird as opposed to the metal foil.

Roast Chicken I *continued*

5 **Place the wrapped bird on a small sheet pan with shallow sides and refrigerate for 3 or 4 days.** This is key to a moist, flavorful chicken. Without this preliminary salting step, the cooked chicken will be dry to a greater or lesser degree.

6 **After three (or four) days, remove the chicken, unwrap it, and discard any accumulated juices. Lightly pat dry inside and out with paper towels.**

Let it come to room temperature, about 45 minutes.

7 **Move the oven rack to the second to bottom position, so the bird will be located in the center of the oven.** If the chicken is too near the top it will tend to burn or cook unevenly from the reflected heat.

8 **Preheat the oven to 300 degrees, not higher. It is essential that the chicken roast at this low 300 degree heat. If the temperature is higher than that, the chicken will dry out over the three-hour cooking time.** Use an accurate oven thermometer to check your oven temperature (see Tips).

9 **Stuff the inside cavity of the bird with the first half of the lemon, then garlic, a bouquet of fresh herbs, and then the last half of the lemon.** We use tarragon, thyme, rosemary, and marjoram. We tie the legs together, but it is optional.

10 **Finely chop 2 tablespoons of thyme, 2 tablespoons of rosemary, 1 tablespoon of tarragon, and mix with 3 tablespoons of olive oil. Add 1 tablespoon of fennel seeds and 1 teaspoon of red pepper flakes** (both of which have been coarsely ground, preferably with a mortar and pestle). Or use herbs of your choice.

11 **Rub the mixture all over the chicken.**

12 **Place the chicken on a bed of fresh herbs of your choice (in place of a rack) on a sheet pan, in an iron skillet, or in a roasting pan.**

13 **Toss the uncooked potatoes with three tablespoons of olive oil, salt and pepper. Arrange them around the chicken.**

14 **Place the chicken near the center of the oven.**

15 **Roast in the oven for 3 hours, basting after 2 hours and turning the potatoes with tongs to brown evenly on both sides.** After 1 ½ hours, you can also turn the chicken pan 180 degrees in the oven to ensure even more uniform cooking.

16 **After cooking, allow the chicken to rest for 10 to 15 minutes before carving.** Serve with the pan juices drizzled over the chicken and the potatoes. This is a truly delicious meal.

Note: Should you have chicken left over, it will make quite an unusual and marvelous chicken salad (see recipe, page 20).

TIPS

We highly recommend using an independent oven thermometer to check the accuracy of your oven temperature. With long-cooking recipes, such as Roast Chicken I (or Baby Back Ribs or Braised Short Ribs), it is essential that the oven is a true 300 degrees since the little chicken will be roasting for three hours. If not true to its setting, your chicken will be dried out.

Roast Chicken II

SERVES 4 TO 6

Depending on how adventurous and perhaps dexterous you are, you may want to use this second version. It has a total cooking time of one hour and has the most wonderfully crisp skin, and because, as in the first version, it has been salted for at least three days (which is absolutely imperative) it is very succulent and tender. It does need more vigilance than the first method because it requires turning every 20 minutes and it needs a careful and steady hand with clean dishtowels in order to turn the chicken accurately.

We think it is worth the extra effort it takes to achieve its final color and texture. The result is magnificent.

1 small high quality roasting chicken, no more than 3 to 4 pounds. A fryer is fine.

Salt, Kosher or sea salt, about 1 tablespoon

Seasoning of choice for the cavity such as thyme, rosemary, tarragon, parsley, several cloves of peeled and smashed garlic, 1 small lemon cut in half.

TOOLS

- A heavy-duty Lodge 10-inch cast iron skillet or other heavy metal pan that will just hold the chicken (see Tip 2)
- Two dish towels (or two silicone mitts) to grab and turn the chicken on its sides. We suggest using two clean, but not fancy, towels designated just for this type of action. This will allow you to firmly position the chicken in the skillet on each of its sides with one confident movement each time you turn it. (We always have two such towels hanging on the stove handle outside the oven for picking up hot pans, hot chickens, or wrapping the handle of a hot pan just set aside as a warning not to touch)
- A wooden spoon. For those less comfortable with the towel technique described above, you can insert the stalk end of a wooden spoon in the cavity of the chicken and rotate the body with the other hand at the head end of the chicken. You will still need to use a dishtowel to protect the one hand from the heat at the head of the chicken
- A small sheet pan, parchment paper and tin foil

1 **Remove all innards from the chicken and discard.**

2 **Rinse chicken thoroughly, inside and out, pat very dry with paper towels.**

3 **Salt chicken all over, using about ¾ teaspoon for each pound of chicken.** Coat thoroughly and evenly over the entire chicken.

4 **Wrap the chicken loosely first with parchment paper and then loosely with a second wrapping of foil.** Although the parchment is optional, we prefer it against the skin of the bird as opposed to metal foil.

5 **Place the wrapped bird on a sheet pan with shallow sides and refrigerate for 3 or 4 days.** This is key to a moist, flavorful chicken. Without this preliminary salting step the cooked chicken will be dry to a greater or lesser degree.

6 **After three or four days, remove the chicken and discard any accumulated juices and lightly pat dry inside and out with paper towels.** Let it come to room temperature, about 45 minutes.

7 **Move the oven rack to the second to bottom position so the chicken will be located in the center of the oven.** If it is too near the top it will tend to burn or cook unevenly from the reflected heat.

8 **Preheat the oven to 475 to 500 degrees (we prefer 500 degrees) and place the skillet in which you will cook the chicken in the oven to preheat it as well.**

9 **Stuff the cavity first with one lemon half, then with herbs of your choice, the garlic, and finally the other half of the lemon** (see Tip 3).

10 **When the oven has reached 475 to 500 degrees remove the preheated skillet or oven-safe pan from the oven and place on top of the stove.**

Roast Chicken II *continued*

11 **Holding the chicken as you would a football from both ends, firmly place one of its sides on the bottom of the skillet, while at the same time making sure its back is right against the side of the skillet so it is propped up and will not fall over.** The skillet should be so hot that when the chicken touches its surface, you hear a searing or hissing sound. If you place the chicken on its back or front and try to roll it on its side or move it much, it will stick to the pan, tearing the skin (see Tip 4).

12 **Place bird and pan on the oven rack.**

13 **After 10 minutes cooking, but no sooner, give the lower portion of the chicken a shove with a wooden spoon or other device.** This prevents the chicken from sticking to the pan.

14 **Roast the chicken on its first side for 20 minutes. After 20 minutes, slide the pan out** (we put it on top of the stove and close the oven door temporarily) **and turn the bird over to the other side.**

15 **Roast for another 20 minutes,** making sure the bird is propped up on its second side.

16 **Finally, turn the chicken breast side up for an additional 15 to 20 minutes or until the skin is a dark brown.** Total cooking time should be about 50 minutes to an hour. (Usually a 3 ½ pound bird cooks in about 60 minutes. Adjust the timings according to oven variation and size of the bird.) The bird is done when the thickest part of the thigh reads 165 to 170 degrees or when the juices run clear, not red or pink, when you tip the chicken or pierce the thigh.

17 **Remove bird from the oven. Allow the bird to rest 10 to 15 minutes or so before carving.** This will allow the juices to be absorbed into the meat.

We find this to be as tender, juicy, and succulent a chicken as we have ever eaten.

TIPS

1. The benefit of a high oven temperature in cooking chicken is that it will cook the leg and thigh before the breast can overcook. Further, the bird will roast, not steam, leaving the skin beautifully crisp.
2. If the pan is much larger than the chicken, the juices will be exposed and could burn and the chicken itself will tend to steam, not roast. Use a heavy-duty cast iron skillet just slightly larger than the chicken.
3. If for some reason you do not wish to stuff the chicken, with herbs, garlic, and lemon, then truss the chicken to prevent the cavity from overheating and cooking the breast from the inside.
4. Use two kitchen towels to firmly grab the bird at both ends. Don't be timid, but grab the bird firmly as though you really mean it and flip it over. It is not hard but one must attack it vigorously.

   For those less comfortable with the towel technique described above, you can insert the stalk end of a wooden spoon in the cavity of the chicken and rotate the body with the other hand at the head end of the chicken. You will still need to use a dishtowel to protect the one hand from the heat at the head of the chicken.
5. We always have two towels hanging on the stove handle outside the oven for picking up hot pans, hot chickens, or wrapping the handle of a hot pan just set aside as a warning not to touch.

FISH

I cook with wine;
sometimes I even add it to the food.

— W.C. FIELDS

Baked Fish with Vegetables

SERVES 4

This is one of our healthiest recipes and it is absolutely delicious and very versatile, to boot. It is equally good regardless of the fish you use. We are illustrating it here with salmon, but feel free to substitute halibut, black sea bass, or tilapia.

Of all the fish and seafood easily available in the United States, salmon in particular is our go-to source of healthy protein. With the addition of three vegetables, it is a complete and very nutritious meal.

Served with Mashed Potatoes (see recipe, page 50), Puréed Cauliflower (see recipe, page 107), or soft polenta, it is one of our favorite dinner party entrées. The plated colors are gorgeous and it is adequately filling so that you do not need a beginning course.

In baking the fish at high temperature, we prefer to use the vegetables as a kind of rack, keeping the fish off the bottom of the scorching pan. The vegetables also add color and additional flavor.

Optionally, we include a glaze below, which we think gives a lovely lacquer to the fish and a refreshing additional flavor complexity.

Our Chicago Cream Sauce (see recipe, page 68) served on the side or spooned over the salmon is a lovely accompaniment to the finished fish if one is not using the glaze.

---

4 five-ounce salmon fillets, preferably Loch Duarte (or halibut, tilapia, or other firm-fleshed white fish)

Kosher salt

Freshly ground black pepper

15 to 20 Cremini (also known as Baby Bellas) or other mushrooms, cleaned and sliced about ¼" inch thick

4 to 6 medium shallots, quartered

1 basket of small tomatoes of your choice, washed and halved or quartered

2 to 3 tablespoons olive oil

Optional Glaze:

3 tablespoons honey

3 to 4 tablespoons Balsamic vinegar

1 teaspoon Dijon-type mustard

Note: For the glaze, you may vary the amounts to taste

TOOLS

- 12-inch stainless steel pan such as an All-Clad
- Metal spatula
- Jar with a lid for the glaze

Optional: Directions for Glaze

In a jar, add good quality honey, such as clover honey, the Balsamic vinegar, and Dijon mustard. Place a lid on the jar and secure tightly. Shake until well-combined. If not using right way, set aside overnight or up to a day in the refrigerator.

Directions for Fish

1 **Take the fish out of the refrigerator 30 minutes before cooking so it reaches room temperature.** Remove any visible pin bones. Season with salt and pepper.

2 **Preheat the oven to 500 degrees.**

3 **Clean and slice the mushrooms about ¼" thick and quarter the shallots. Set aside.**

4 **Cut the tomatoes in half or quarters. Set aside.**

5 **Put the olive oil in the stainless steel pan and heat it until hot.**

6 **Add the shallots and cook for several minutes until soft and on the verge of browning. Add the mushrooms and cook until they are softened.** Add olive oil as needed if the pan becomes a bit dry.

Baked Fish with Vegetables *continued*

7 **Add the tomatoes and evenly spread out the three vegetables over the surface of the pan.**

Optional: For those who love the skin of salmon seared to a dark crispness, as we do, heat 2 tablespoons olive oil and 1 tablespoon butter in an iron mineral or cast iron pan until very hot. Place the fish skin side down and sear for 4 to 5 minutes. Do not try to move it. It will tear. As the skin is cooking, take a spoon and baste the flesh side of the fish with the butter-olive oil several times, cooking the flesh as you baste. Proceed with remainder of recipe but note that the cooking time in the oven will be reduced since the fish is now partially cooked.

8 **Immediately place the salmon filets (or preferred fish) on top of the vegetables.** Optional: At this juncture you can add the glaze, just enough to cover the salmon.

9 **Put the pan in the middle of the oven or a bit higher and cook from 7 to 11 minutes until the fish gives to the pressure of the back of a fork.**

Some of us like our salmon on the rare side, so the time will vary according to your preference for doneness. Halfway through the cooking, you can brush a little more glaze over the fish.

10 **Remove from oven and serve with the vegetables surrounding the fish and covering it.**

TIPS

This recipe can be made a day in advance and served cold as a salad on top of a bed of greens, accompanied by a slice of lemon or an extra dish of vinaigrette or our Chicago Cream Sauce. If crisping the skin as suggested in #7, remove skin before serving the fish cold as a salad.

MEAT

The only time to eat diet food is while you are waiting for the steak to cook.

— JULIA CHILD

Steak–Chicago Style

SERVES 1 TO 2

Who says grilling outdoors is the be-all and end-all of cooking steak? We don't think so anymore. We now cook steak indoors because of the foolproof procedure we present here and our nod to the environment. Although most backyard cooks believe steak is best served from the grill, this indoor method produces a divine result.

We use bone-in rib eye, but one can use any steak of choice such as a New York strip. If taste is a priority, we make sure the steak is marbled with fat, and includes the bone, which we believe improves flavor.

The secret is the quality of the meat and the technique. Let the iron skillet get very, very hot and use neither oil nor butter in the pan. The natural fat in the meat will provide plenty of "oil" once cooking begins and the fat starts to render. If the iron skillet is hot enough and the steak is left undisturbed on its first side, it will never stick to the pan and it will develop a beautiful crust.

We suggest serving the steak with Classic Onion Rings (see recipe, page 65), or French Fries--RM Style (see recipe, page 48), and a green vegetable, such as Seared Asparagus (see recipe, page 66), or even Creamed Spinach (see recipe, page 58).

One steak. Our favorite is bone-in rib eye. Use 1" or 1 ¼" thick steaks (no thicker) as if too much thicker than that, they will not cook through evenly

Kosher salt

Pepper

TOOLS

- Heavy, 12-inch Lodge cast iron skillet, no other pan type, including older, thinner cast iron (see Tip 2)
- Spatula or tongs
- Very good exhaust fan

1 **Take the steak out of the refrigerator and pat dry with paper towels.** Then let sit for 45 minutes or so on fresh paper towels to further dry and reach room temperature before cooking (see Tips 3 and 4).

2 **Heat the cast iron skillet on low heat for about 10 minutes and let it get warm** (see Tip 6).

3 **Then turn up the flame to high for about 4 to 5 minutes until the pan is extremely hot and smoking.** Do not skip this step as it is essential for a great indoor steak. Most home cooks are afraid to allow a thick cast iron pan to get hot enough. Do not fall into this trap. Use no oil or butter. Turn your exhaust fan on very high as the searing meat will create a lot of smoke.

4 **After about 4 minutes, sprinkle the pan with salt, lightly covering the bottom.** Let the pan get very hot, a total of about 5 minutes.

5 **Place the steak in the pan and leave it alone.** If you heated the pan correctly the meat should make a definite hissing sound upon contact with the pan. Do not move it and do not push it around or press down with your spatula or tongs.

6 **Sear the meat for about 4 minutes on the first side.** Doing this allows a tasty crust to form, which will easily release from the pan.

7 **Flip the steak over on the second side** (see Tip 7).

8 **After a minute or so, turn the flame down to medium high.** Cook the second side for about 3 to 4 minutes for rare, and longer for medium or well. Judgment is required on degree of doneness and you get the hang of it from experience (see Tip 8).

9 **Remove the steak from the pan and put on a cutting board or other suitable platform.**

Allow the meat to rest, which is said to allow the juices to distribute, tented with some tin foil to help keep it warm. While much is said about meat resting after cooking, in our experience we have not found a noticeable difference between allowing a steak to rest and carving it immediately.

Note: If you leave the steak to rest after cooking then it will cook more on its own, called carry-over cooking. Learn how long to cook any meat, fish, baked goods, or vegetables, taking into account carry-over cooking.

TIPS

1. Always pat the meat surface dry before cooking. This prevents the meat from steaming rather than searing. We simply use paper towels to remove any moisture from the surface of the meat before seasoning it.
2. When cooking steak or any meat such as hamburger, lamb burger, or lamb chops, use a heavy cast iron skillet. You want a pan that can take very high heat and produce a good sear. We never ever use any pan to sear meat other than a good, thick cast iron skillet. Don't even think about using a nonstick skillet for this purpose. We use a Lodge 12-inch cast iron skillet for cooking meat at high temperature as it is very heavy and thick unlike older, smoother cast iron which is thinner and doesn't take abuse and high heat as well as the Lodge. However, the older cast iron (Griswold and Wagner) is wonderful for lower heat situations as it's smoother surface acts more like a nonstick surface.
3. Either season the steak with pepper to taste as it is coming to room temperature or wait until the steak has cooked a few minutes. We prefer pepper applied at once before cooking starts, as it tends to burn and crust on the steak this way. Add no salt to the steak, as the pan will be salted before cooking.
4. If you wish you can use ground pepper (or use a mortar and pestle on fresh pepper corns for the best flavor) and cover one side of the steak with crushed peppercorns. Push the pepper in with your hand. You now have a version of the famous steak au poivre. Delicious.
5. When you are through cooking the meat, let the pan cool down some, then coat it with a high temp oil such as grapeseed, coconut, or peanut oil. If bits of meat are still on the surface scrape them off with a thin wooden spatula, a thin plastic scraper, or a small chain mail made for this purpose, being careful the surface isn't too hot. Then once relatively clean, wipe the pan with a paper towel so a thin sheen of oil is left.
6. When cooking with any metal pan, try and first warm the skillet up for 10 minutes, as this prevents warping from the sudden high heat that will be required in cooking meat. When warmed up, turn up the flame to high until the skillet is very, very hot, at least for 4 to 5 minutes. This will produce a wonderful sear and crust on the meat and the meat won't stick to the pan, even without oil or butter. Just use a light sprinkling of salt on the pan during the last minute of heating.
7. If you wish, you can sear the fat on the edges of the steak by turning the steak on its end(s) and either holding it with tongs or balancing it against the side of the skillet. This will give the steak a nice finish and for those who like to eat the fat, it will taste much better. This can be done when you first put the steak in the pan or at the very end, but watch carefully as this will cook the steak a bit more.
8. One of the best ways to judge doneness is to use a high quality thermometer slipped into the side of the meat and moved into the center of the cut. Do not touch the bone or the pan with the tip of the thermometer. **Rare:** 120 to 130 degrees. **Medium rare:** 135 degrees. **Medium:** 140 degrees. **Well done:** 145 to 150 degrees (beyond that, the meat will be tougher than an elephant's hide).

Seared Roast Beef

SERVES 3 TO 4

This is clearly the most delicious red meat we have ever tasted. Our friends and testers seem to agree and we hope you will, too. The combination of the cut of meat and this special, exacting technique creates an irresistible result. To achieve it, you must follow the instructions below precisely and without variation.

We were familiar with the traditional cooking of standing rib roast and had cooked and eaten it many times both at home and in restaurants, but strangely, we were never thrilled by it.

Then one winter night, a power outage during a Chicago storm forced Jonathan to use a piece of roast beef he had on hand so it would not spoil or go to waste as it was now involuntarily defrosting. Having no choice, he used the fat, 2 ½" thick piece of meat with bone and began cooking it as one does a steak (see recipe, page 34) in a very hot cast iron skillet. Due to its thickness, it was raw after the usual cooking time, 4 to 5 minutes on a side, so he finished the meat in a 500-degree oven. The result was magical: a juicy, tender inside with a very crisp outside.

The secret is the quality of meat, its exact thickness, and the technique described here. One must let the iron skillet get very hot and not use oil or butter in the pan. The natural fat in the meat will provide plenty of "oil" once cooking begins. If the iron skillet is hot enough and the bone-in rib eye cut is left undisturbed on its first side, it will never stick to the pan and more importantly, it will develop a delicious crust.

One cut of meat from a standing rib roast of the highest quality, with its own bone. One piece of standing rib roast serves about three people or two pieces for six people and so on. Each piece must be about 2 ¼" to 2 ½" thick and is essentially an overly thick bone-in rib eye. You will not find this cut in your butcher's meat display case, although there is a similar cut referred to as a Tomahawk steak. We insist on a fresh cut of the exact right size. The desired piece must be cut away from a standing rib roast with one bone intact for each piece of meat. Do not let the butcher give you a normal bone-in rib eye steak from the display case, which is normally about 1¼" thick as it is not thick enough for this recipe

Kosher salt

Pepper

TOOLS

- A Lodge heavy-duty 12-inch cast iron skillet (no other, including older, thinner cast iron.)
- Spatula or tongs
- Very good exhaust fan

1 **Take the roast beef out of the refrigerator** a good hour before cooking so it reaches room temperature.

2 **Pat it dry with paper towels on both sides.** Let it sit on paper towels coming to room temperature. Season with pepper only, no salt, as the pan will be salted before cooking. If you wish, you can add the pepper later after the meat has cooked several minutes. We prefer the pepper somewhat crusted and burnt, so we apply it before cooking.

3 **Turn on the oven to 500 degrees.**

4 **First warm the cast iron skillet on low heat for about 10 minutes.** (This lets the metal warm up without the shock of immediate high heat.)

5 **Then turn the heat to high for about 4 to 5 minutes until the pan is extremely hot and smoking.** Do not skip this part as it is the essential first step for a great piece of meat. Most cooks are afraid to allow a pan to get hot enough. Don't fall into this trap. Use no oil or butter. Turn your exhaust fan on very high as the searing meat will create a lot of smoke.

6 **Sprinkle the pan with salt, covering the bottom slightly but consistently.** Let the salt heat up another minute.

7 **Place the dry meat in the pan and leave it alone.** If you heated the pan correctly the meat should make a definite hissing sound upon contact with the pan. Do not move it and do not push it down with your spatula or tongs

8 **Sear the meat for about 4 to 5 minutes on the first side.** Doing this allows a crust to form, which will easily release from the pan.

9 Flip the meat over on the second side. Turn the heat down to medium-high. Cook the second side for about 4 to 5 minutes.

For a nice extra touch, and one we suggest in the case of seared roast beef, you can sear the fat on the narrow sides of the meat by turning it on its ends and leaning it against the side of the pan or holding it with tongs in an upright position. Do this for all fatty sides you wish to sear. This creates both a gorgeous looking and tasting piece of meat.

10 Transfer the meat to the middle of the oven in the same cast iron skillet, and roast at 500 degrees for 10 to 16 minutes. Judgment is required on degree of doneness and one gets the hang of it from experience. Using a meat thermometer is the most accurate way.

Rare: 120 to 130 degrees. **Medium rare:** 135 degrees. Medium: 140 degrees. **Well done:** 145 to 150 or above. But remember if you leave the meat to rest after cooking then it will cook more on its own so adjust accordingly, that is, 120 to 130 degrees will be a good medium rare instead of rare.

11 Remove the meat from the pan and put it on a cutting board or other suitable platform. Allow it to rest (said to allow juices to distribute) tented with some tin foil to help keep it warm.

We normally serve by cutting the meat into slices for our guests at the table. Give the bone to those who wish it. One piece of the meat with bone serves 3 to 4 people.

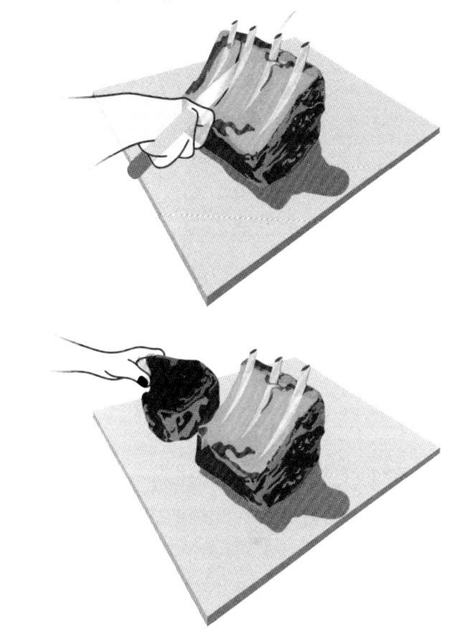

TIPS

1. If you wish you can add the pepper later after the meat has cooked several minutes. In that way it won't burn or crust so much during cooking. We prefer the pepper somewhat crusted and burnt so we apply it before cooking.
2. When cooking seared roast beef or any meat such as hamburger, lamb burger, lamb chops use a heavy cast iron skillet. You want a pan that can take very high heat and produce a good sear. We never ever use any pan to sear meat other than a good heavy-duty cast iron skillet. Do not even think about using a nonstick skillet for this purpose. We use a Lodge 12-inch cast iron skillet for cooking meat at high temperature as it is very heavy and thick unlike older, smoother cast iron which is thinner and doesn't take abuse and high heat as well as the Lodge. However, the older cast iron (Griswold and Wagner) is wonderful for lower heat situations as it's smoother surface acts more like a nonstick surface (see Techniques and Equipment, page 116).

About Roast Beef

Prime Roast of Beef is a gift from our English and Irish forbearers and founders of our country. Often called a Standing Rib Roast, it is traditionally served with Yorkshire pudding, horseradish sauce, and gravy. Beginning in the mid-19th century, it became a Sunday dinner staple, eaten at noon after church services.

These days, such cuts of beef are for a special occasion meal, since they are pricey.

Baby Back Ribs—Chicago Style

ONE RACK SERVES 1 TO 2 PEOPLE

In one sense, these are not really ribs at all, but gourmet pork, attached to bones. And they may be the ultimate comfort food. Surely, every person who has tasted these ribs has found them irresistible.

We normally serve them only on key occasions including elegant dinner parties; they are that special. To add to the joy, they can, and really should, be made a day ahead of schedule and simply heated up for serving or when it is convenient. As with many foods, they taste better the next day.

The basics of this recipe were passed down to us by an old-school cook and dear friend from the South Side of Chicago. We have followed her recipe with minor refinements.

The recipe can be varied in taste depending on the rub used and the barbecue sauce. We use bottled Sweet Baby Ray's Original Barbecue Sauce as it is delicious, especially with the addition of fresh orange juice, and it is easily available. The rub we use is put together here in Chicago at the Spice House, and is called Bronzeville Rib Rub. We know cooks have their favorite rubs and sauces and you should use the ones you prefer, but you will be hard pressed to do better than Sweet Baby Ray's Original Barbecue Sauce with the addition of fresh orange juice and a good rub.

What gives these ribs character is the slow, 12 to 14-hour long cooking process which tenderizes the meat and cooks off the oily fat. So plan ahead. Once cooked, you can easily reheat and serve whenever convenient.

1 18-ounce bottle of Sweet Baby Ray's Original Barbecue Sauce for two racks of ribs

About ½ cup or more (preferably fresh) orange juice to taste if using 18 oz of Sweet Baby Ray's sauce. Too much orange juice and it will thin the sauce too much and be too sweet

Optional: ⅛ teaspoon cayenne pepper to taste

1 to 3 slabs of baby back ribs (6 to 8 ribs will serve one person)

Rib rub

TOOLS

- Large baking pan
- Large tongs, preferably with silicone coated ends to avoid tearing up the meat.
- Spoon, spatula or brush for the BBQ sauce.
- Heavy-duty tin foil
- Parchment paper

Directions for Sauce

Mix an 18-ounce bottle of Sweet Baby Ray's Original Barbecue Sauce with about ½ to 1 cup of orange juice, to taste. Stir well. Add a touch of cayenne if you want to spice things up a bit. Refrigerate until ready to use, preferably overnight so the flavors marry up.

Or use your favorite BBQ sauce.

Directions for Ribs

1 **Cover a large sheet pan with heavy-duty aluminum foil.**

2 **Cut a length of parchment paper large enough to fold around and under each rack of ribs.**

3 **Put the rack of ribs on the parchment and sprinkle and rub both sides of the ribs with dry rub as one would somewhat liberally salt meat, about 1 teaspoon per side per rack.** Do not apply it too thickly or the rub will overwhelm the flavor of the ribs.

4 **Fold and close parchment paper somewhat loosely around one of the rib slabs, covering completely, but not pressing down heavily into the rub and meat.** Seam side should be up.

5 **Then cut a length of heavy-duty foil and fold it somewhat loosely, but completely around the parchment and loosely seal.** Keep the seam side up. In this way the barbecue sauce and fatty juices will not run out onto the pan. Do this for each slab of ribs.

6 **Put the pan of ribs into a preheated oven at 180 degrees for about 12 to 14 hours** (see Tip 1).

7 **When ribs have fully cooked, remove from the oven** (see Tip 2).

8 **Gently lift the wrapped ribs off the pan onto a plate or other surface.** Let them cool so they won't fall apart so easily when handled.

9 **When cooled, unwrap the ribs and, using tongs or another suitable instrument, lift them out of the parchment and back onto the tin foil-lined pan, bone side up.**

10 **Cover the ribs on the bone side with a medium thick layer of sauce using a spoon, spatula, or brush.**

11 **Put in a broiler. Caramelize until the bone side is a rich brown/black color, about 3 to 5 minutes.** Take care not to burn the ribs (see Tip 3).

12 **Take the ribs out of the oven and turn them over (bone side down). Spread a medium thick layer of sauce on the meaty side.**

13 **Put back in the oven and broil for about 3 to 5 minutes or until you have a deep brown or nearly black caramelized crust.** It is the creation of this caramelized crust of sauce that helps give the ribs great flavor and a contrasting texture of crunch foiled against the soft inner meat.

14 **Either serve at once or, better yet, let cool, cover, and refrigerate.** The flavors will marry up over the hours or overnight. Heat up later, or the next day, in a nonstick or nonreactive pan, right on top of the stove, adding a bit more sauce to keep the ribs moist and flavorful. And you can heat up the extra leftover sauce separately for those who wish more sauce on their ribs, and many will.

Serve with Coleslaw (see recipe, page 62) and Applesauce (see recipe, page 60).

Optional:
Quasi Memphis Pulled Pork Sandwich: For an amazing alternative, pull or cut the meat off the bones and serve on a bun (we prefer a pretzel bun or brioche bun, but some prefer plain white bread) topped with Coleslaw (see recipe, page 62) and a little more warmed sauce. Add another bun on top if you wish. True comfort food.

TIPS

1. It is particularly important when cooking food for a long period of time that the oven temperature is accurate. Preheat the oven for 30 minutes or more and check that the temperature is at 180 degrees with a high quality oven thermometer. If too high or too low, compensate as needed when you cook the ribs. If too high, it is easy to dry out the ribs from overcooking. Err on the low side.
2. Degree of doneness is a matter of preference. The longer you cook the ribs the more the meat will fall off the bone. (If cooked too long the meat will dry out.) Some like to pull the meat off the bone with their teeth, in which case cook the ribs less, 12 or so hours. We like the meat falling off the bone and we like to eat it with a fork and knife. Hence we cook the ribs closer to 14 hours. It is something one has to get a feel for due to different oven temperatures and pans and taste.
3. Since you will be cooking the ribs in the middle part of the oven for 12 to 14 hours, when it comes time to broil them, do not forget to move the rack up to around 6 inches from the broiler. Too close and they will burn. Too far away and they will not brown properly.
4. To lift such tender ribs, use a long pair of rubber-tipped tongs and slip one of the arms of the tongs completely under the rib rack, lengthwise. Gently pinch the whole rack by squeezing down on the other tong, gripping the rib rack down its length. Then lift them straight up.

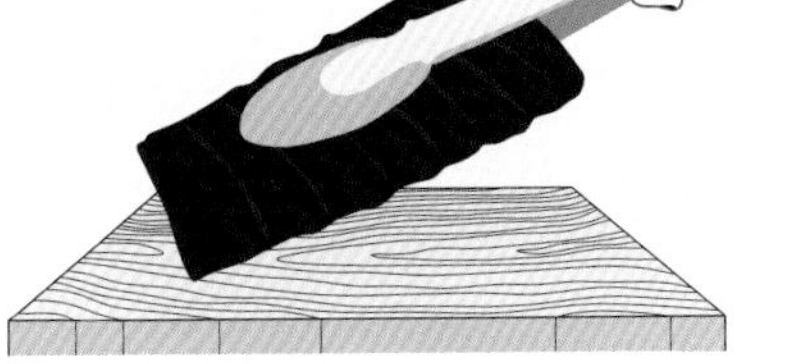

Hamburger

SERVES 1 PATTY PER PERSON

A hamburger prepared with an exact method will acquire gourmet status, better than those served in most high-end restaurants, and as good as any meat you will taste.

The secret is the quality of meat and this simple, but precise technique described in the directions below.

Most of our friends and acquaintances prefer the taste of a burger cooked in this way to the alternative, outdoor grilling.

As with any burger, it is important to handle the meat as little as possible since it is the over-kneading of the meat that will toughen the finished burger and prevent the juices from flowing internally during cooking.

1 pound coarsely ground sirloin or coarsely ground grass fed beef, chuck, short ribs, brisket, or your choice of any of these cuts mixed together. Try to get the meat freshly ground that day or even better, ground at the time of purchase by the butcher (it is also safer). If you wish full flavor, you will want about 10 to 20% fat content so have the butcher grind in some fat with the meat as needed. The more well-done you like your meat (which also makes it safer to eat, but less flavorful) the more you will want a higher fat content

Frankly, and unlike many hamburger experts, we prefer ground sirloin, as it is delicious and simple to purchase

Kosher salt

Pepper

TOOLS

- Heavy, 12-inch (or larger if cooking more than two burgers) Lodge cast iron skillet (no other pan type, including older, thinner cast iron)
- Spatula

1 **Take the meat out of the refrigerator and let it come to room temperature, about 30 to 45 minutes.**

2 **Make each burger by gently creating a patty using about ¼ pound of meat.** Do not handle the meat excessively. Each patty should be about ¾ of an inch thick (see Tip 1).

3 **Before cooking, thoroughly dry the meat with paper towels so it sears well** (if wet, it will tend to steam).

3 **Meanwhile, warm the thick cast iron skillet on low heat for about 10 minutes.** This lets the metal warm up without the shock of immediate high heat.

5 **Then turn the flame up to high for about 4 to 5 minutes until the pan is extremely hot and smoking.** Do not skip this part as it is the essential first step for a great indoor burger. Most cooks are afraid to allow a cast iron pan to get hot enough. Do not fall into this trap. Use no oil or butter. Turn your exhaust fan on very high as the searing meat will create a lot of smoke.

6 **After some 4 minutes, sprinkle the pan with salt, covering the bottom slightly, but consistently.** Let the salt heat up another minute.

7 **Place the burger in the pan and leave it alone.** It should make an audible searing sound upon contact with the pan if the pan is hot enough. Do not move it and do not push it down with your spatula. If you are cooking three or more burgers, be sure to use a large enough pan so the burgers have space between them so they sear and not steam.

8 **Sear the meat for about 3 to 4 minutes on the first side.** Doing this allows a crust to form and the burger will easily release from the pan if you leave it in place and do not push it around or down.

9 **Flip the burger over on the second side and turn the flame down to medium high.** Cook the second side for about 3 to 4 minutes for rare. Judgment is required here and one will get the hang of how long to cook the burger depending on the thickness of the meat, the pan, and the height of the flame (see Tip 3).

10 **Remove the burger from the pan.** You can let the meat rest before serving under a foil tent, which is said to redistribute the juices, but will allow the burger to cook more.

Serve alone or on a bun, single piece of Pan-Fried Toast (see recipe, page 56), and/or with The Fried Egg on top (see recipe, page 78).

TIPS

1. If the patty is too thick, it will not cook evenly leaving a rare portion in the middle. If too thin it will over-cook before you get a good sear. You can use your thumb to press down and make a ½ inch indentation into the center of the raw patty, which will promote more even cooking.
2. If you plan to cook your meat to the safe temperature of 160 degrees you can put in a chunk of butter, optionally with garlic mixed into it, and fold gently into the hamburger when first preparing it. As the burger cooks, the butter melts and helps keep the meat juicy despite being very well-done.
3. The best way to determine doneness is to use a high quality thermometer inserted into the side of the burger and pushed in toward the center of the patty. **Rare:** 120 to 130 degrees. **Medium rare:** 135 degrees. **Medium:** 140 degrees. **Well done:** 145 to 150 or above. But remember, if you let the burger rest after cooking, then it will cook more on its own, so adjust accordingly. That is, 120 to 130 degrees will be a good medium rare instead of rare .
4. When you are through cooking the burger, let the pan cool down some, then coat it thinly with high-temperature oil such as grapeseed, coconut, or peanut. If bits of burger are still on the surface scrape them off with a thin plastic scraper or a chain mail scraper made for this purpose, being careful the surface is not too hot. Then once relatively clean, wipe the pan with a paper towel so a thin sheen of oil is left.

About the Hamburger

It is truly interesting that two of America's favorite sandwiches, the hamburger and the frankfurter (or hot dog) were named for cities in Germany, yet were developed right here in our country. Further, they both became famous at World Fairs. The hot dog gained recognition at the Columbian Exposition of 1893 in Chicago and the hamburger became popular at the St. Louis World Fair in 1904. See our Chicago hot dog interview (page 101) elsewhere in this book.

We see hamburger-like dishes in other world cultures, such as the famous French table-side presentation of steak tartar, where raw ground steak is prepared with egg, herbs, and mustard and served as a first course. The kebab of the Middle East is a hamburger-like preparation using ground beef or lamb.

Perhaps the reason the hamburger's popularity came about was due to the industrialized life of the early 20th century, the quickness of its preparation, and the fact that busy lives prevented home cooks from spending as much time in meat preparation as was once expected. It is surely now one of the iconic dishes of American life.

Lamb Burger

SERVES 1 PATTY PER PERSON

When it comes to the burger, we love lamb burgers as much as hamburgers. Truly, lamb is such a delicacy and yet often it is shunned in this country except on certain holidays. Many people are afraid of lamb because of its high fat content, but that is exactly what gives it such a rich flavor. Do not underestimate this wonderful and unusual burger.

If lamb in burger form is unfamiliar to your menu repertoire, do not shortchange it. Lamb burgers are a delicious and sophisticated departure from the ubiquitous hamburger. We often serve these as the main meal at dinner parties on a piece of Pan-Fried Toast (see recipe, page 56) using artisan Italian bread or with an egg on top.

As with any burger, it is important to handle the meat as little as possible since handling will toughen the finished burger.

1 pound fresh, ground lamb, ¼ pound per person

Kosher salt

Pepper

TOOLS

- Heavy, 12-inch (or larger if cooking more than three burgers) Lodge cast iron skillet (no other pan type, including older thinner cast iron such as Griswold and Wagner)
- Spatula

1 **Take the meat out of the refrigerator and let it come to room temperature for about 30 to 45 minutes.**

2 **Make each burger by gently creating a patty using about ¼ pound of meat.** Each patty should be about ¾ of an inch thick.

3 **Before cooking, thoroughly dry the meat with paper towels so it sears well** (if wet, it will tend to steam).

4 **Meanwhile, warm the cast iron skillet on low heat for about 10 minutes.** This allows the metal to warm up without the shock of immediate high heat.

5 **Then turn the flame up to high for about 4 to 5 minutes until the pan is extremely hot and smoking.** Do not skip this part as it is the essential first step for a great indoor burger. Most cooks are afraid to allow a cast iron pan to get hot enough. Do not fall into this trap. Use no oil or butter. Turn your exhaust fan on very high as the searing meat will create a lot of smoke.

6 **After some 4 minutes, sprinkle the pan with salt, covering the bottom slightly, but consistently.** Let the salt heat up another minute.

7 **Place the burger in the pan and leave it alone.** It should make an audible searing sound upon contact with the pan if the pan is hot enough. Do not move it and do not push it down with your spatula. If you are cooking three or more burgers, be sure to use a large enough pan so the burgers have space between them, searing, not steaming the meat.

8 **Sear the meat for about 3 to 4 minutes on the first side.** Doing this allows a crust to form and the burger will easily release from the pan if you don't mess with it.

9 Flip the lamb burger over on the second side and turn the flame down to medium high. Cook the second side for about 3 to 4 minutes for rare. Judgment is required here and one will get the hang of how long to cook the burger depending on the thickness of the meat, the pan, and the height of the flame (see Tip 3).

10 Remove the burger from the pan. You can let the meat rest before serving under a foil tent, which is said to redistribute the juices, but will allow the burger to cook more.

Serve alone or on a bun, single piece of Pan-Fried Toast (see recipe, page 56), or with The Fried Egg on top (see recipe, page 78).

TIPS

1. If the patty is too thick, it will not cook evenly leaving a rarer portion in the middle. If too thin it will over-cook. You can use your thumb to press down and make a ½ inch indentation into the center of the patty, which will promote more even cooking.
2. If you plan to cook your meat to the safe temperature of 160 degrees you can put in a chunk of butter and fold gently into the lamb burger. As the burger cooks, the butter melts and helps keep the meat juicy despite being very well done.
3. The best way to determine doneness is to use a high quality thermometer inserted into the side of the burger and pushed in toward the center of the patty. **Rare:** 120 to 130 degrees. **Medium rare:** 135 degrees. **Medium:** 140 degrees. **Well done:** 145 to 150 or above. But remember, if you let the burger rest after cooking, then it will cook more on its own, so adjust accordingly. That is, 120 to 130 degrees will be a good medium rare instead of rare.
4. When you are through cooking the burger, let the pan cool down some, then coat it thinly with a high temperature oil such as grapeseed, coconut, or peanut. If bits of burger are still on the surface scrape them off with a thin plastic scraper or chain mail scraper made for this purpose, being careful the surface is not too hot. Then once relatively clean, wipe the pan with a paper towel so a thin sheen of oil is left.

Braised Short Ribs

SERVES 2 TO 3 RIBS PER PERSON

If succulent and unctuous meat dishes appeal to you, this delicious recipe meets both of those criteria and it isn't even pork! We love slow and low cooked meat, be it pork, beef or chicken. We experimented with this dish until we had it just right. The nice part about this recipe is that it is easy to prepare and you can go about your life while the ribs braise away for five hours. The low and slow cooking combined makes for fall-off-the-bone meat, free of the stringiness that often occurs with this cut of beef, surely the result from having been cooked for too brief a time. It is the five hours and low oven temperature that gives the meat the juicy, richness it achieves.

We have chosen to braise these short ribs in a rich, tangy, made-from-scratch barbecue sauce. Make the sauce a day in advance to allow its flavors to develop and to make your preparation more relaxed. Half the sauce is used to braise the cooking ribs and the rest of the sauce is heated up later to serve with the ribs.

We suggest serving this with Coleslaw (page 62), Potato Salad (page 52), or Applesauce (page 60). Potato Latkes (page 54) or Mashed Potatoes (page 50) are both delicious with this as well.

This is rich, hearty eating, perfect for cold weather.

Ingredients for Sauce

1 ½ cups balsamic vinegar, or to taste

½ cup orange vinegar

1 medium red onion, diced

14 cloves of garlic, minced

4 tablespoons orange juice

2 cups ketchup

12 ounces beer

½ cup honey

6 tablespoons grainy mustard

2 tablespoons molasses

2 tablespoons hoisin sauce (we prefer Koon Chun)

3 teaspoons Worcestershire sauce

1 teaspoon cayenne, or to taste

6 grinds of black pepper

2 teaspoons dried thyme

2 tablespoons dry sherry

½ cup dark brown sugar, or to taste

4 teaspoons salt

½ cup water

TOOLS FOR SAUCE

- Le Creuset sauté pan with a large surface area (12 inches or more in diameter)
  We prefer the wide deep sauté pan made by Le Creuset with its enamel finish and large, skillet-like surface area, but any good high quality saucier or saucepan will do, such as All-Clad. In this case, a larger pan is beneficial for reducing the sauce, but not essential. (A saucier has sloping sides, allowing effective whisking of the sauce)
- A wooden paddle (we use those made by Michael Ruhlman) or a heatproof silicone spatula both of which are better for scraping the bottom and sides of a pan than a wooden or heatproof spoon (see Tip 2)
- Glass storage jars

Directions for Sauce

(Note: the below recipe for sauce is the same recipe as our Sweet and Sour Barbecue Sauce (page 70), but we doubled the amounts here for use with the braised short ribs.)

This an unusual recipe in that the majority of the process is *mise en place*, the French cooking technique that calls for all of the ingredients in a recipe to be measured and assembled before beginning to cook. While the vinegars are reducing, we highly recommend carrying out the *mise en place* as it will be a much easier recipe to put together.

Because the short ribs braise for five hours, the sauce tends to cook down quite a bit and the fat from the short ribs renders into the sauce during cooking. This of course adds wonderful flavor to the meat.

After five hours, remove the ribs from the pan and set them aside. We recommend discarding the sauce in which the meat braised. Then heat the remaining (untouched) half of the sauce and serve over the ribs.

1 **Place the balsamic and orange vinegars in a large non-reactive skillet or saucepan, place on a diffuser if possible, and bring to a gentle boil over medium heat.**

2 **Then reduce the flame a bit and cook at a good simmer (small bubbles) until it is reduced by a third, which should take about 30 to 40 minutes.**

Do this step in a well-ventilated room since the fumes at first are quite strong, though neither toxic nor dangerous.

3 **While the vinegars reduce, prepare all of the remaining ingredients which is called *mise en place*** (see Tip 1).

4 **When the vinegars are reduced, add all of the remaining ingredients along with ½ cup water.** Stir to combine well with a wooden or silicone paddle, scraping the bottom of the pan well.

5 **Bring back to a small boil, then reduce the heat to medium low or so, and simmer until thick, 30 to 40 minutes.**

6 **If the sauce becomes too thick, add a little water.**

7 **Adjust to taste by adding more vinegar, or salt and pepper.**

8 **When complete, pour into glass jars and cool before refrigerating overnight to allow the flavors to marry.**

Makes about 6 cups.

Ingredients for Short Ribs

3 to 4 tablespoons olive oil

6 beef short ribs, NOT cross cut, but block short ribs, two or three ribs per person

Salt and pepper

Sweet and sour barbecue sauce (see recipe, page 44)

TOOLS FOR SHORT RIBS

- Large Dutch oven such as a Le Creuset pan or pot with lid
- Large tongs

Directions for Short Ribs

1 **Preheat the oven to 225 degrees.**

2 **On the stove top, heat oil in a large Dutch oven such as a Le Creuset pot until hot, but not smoking.**

3 **Sear short ribs thoroughly on all sides, salt and peppering them.** If all the ribs cannot fit in the pan at one time, sear them in batches, setting them aside.

4 **Pour off all the accumulated fat and put the ribs back into the pan.**

5 **Pour half of the barbecue sauce over the ribs to almost cover. Put the remaining half of the sauce in the refrigerator in a glass jar.**

6 **Cover the pan with the lid and place in the 225 degree oven.**

7 **Braise for a full five hours, turning the ribs over once if you wish.** They are done when the meat is falling off the bone. Discard the sauce in which you braised the ribs. If serving the next day, which we recommend, see Tips 4 and 5.

8 **Heat the remainder, second half, of the sauce** (from the refrigerator) **in a saucepan and serve over the ribs.**

Braised Short Ribs *continued*

TIPS

1. *Mise en place* is a French term used by chefs to refer to the preparation of all ingredients before beginning any recipe. Each ingredient is placed in its own prep bowl and assembled on a cutting board or suitable surface. As you follow the recipe directions, each ingredient has been measured and gathered in one place, making your cooking more accurate and more efficient. If you get in the habit of doing the *mise en place* each time you cook, you will see its advantage.
2. Through trial and error we found a flat wooden paddle or silicone spatula works much better than a traditional wooden spoon for stirring sauces, soup, or scrambling eggs. The flat surface scrapes up the ingredients much more efficiently. We get our wooden paddles from Michael Ruhlman's website. Silicone spatulas are widely available.
3. When doing any long simmering on the stovetop, we find a diffuser very useful. A diffuser evens out the heat of the gas flame and gives more precise control. You can keep the food at a steady low simmer, spreading the heat evenly throughout the pan or skillet. We use an artisan copper diffuser (made by Bella) that works perfectly, as copper is an excellent conductor of heat.
4. As with many low-and-long cooking meat, serving it the next day allows flavors to blend and meld (called "marrying"), producing a much tastier dish. We recommend it.
5. For overnight storage, place braised ribs in a glass container and spoon some of the fresh, reserved barbecue sauce over them. When cool, cover and refrigerate overnight. When ready to serve the next day, reheat with second half of the sauce. Serve as suggested above.

POTATOES

I have made a lot of mistakes falling in love, and regretted most of them, but never the potatoes that went with them.

— NORA EPHRON

French Fries–RM Style

SERVES 2 TO 3

These fabulous fries taste as good or better than classic French Fries, but are much easier to make.

French fries may have originated in another country (Belgium or France), but they surely have become as American as apple pie.

These fries are a huge hit whenever served because of their unique size, the way they are cut, and the manner in which they are cooked.

We learned the basics of this recipe from a close friend (RM) and with minor variation, created these near perfect fries. The trick is exactly following the technique described below.

1 Large Idaho baking potato or large Yukon Gold (scrubbed but unpeeled)

Olive oil (just enough to cover the bottom of the skillet, and no more)

Salt and pepper

TOOLS

- 12-inch metal skillet (stainless steel by All-Clad, metal mineral pan by de Buyer or cast iron skillet)
- Large metal spatula
- Paper towels

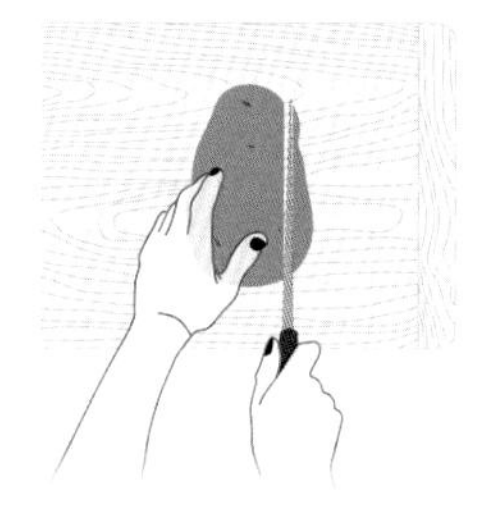

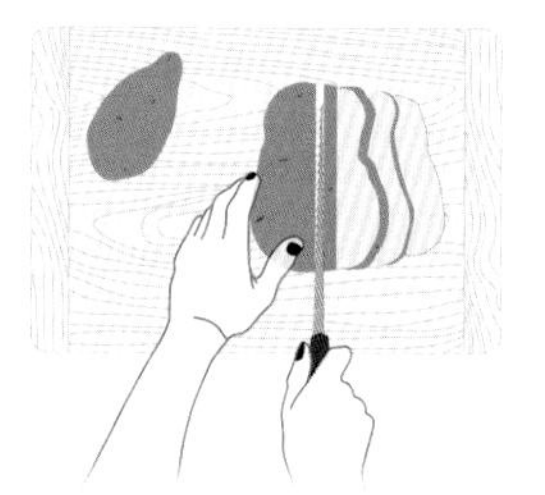

1 **Orient the unpeeled potato lengthwise with one end pointing at your body and one end pointing away from your body. To stabilize the potato, cut one small lengthwise slice off of the potato. Flip the potato onto the flat side.**

2 **With the newly created flat side down, cut slices the full length of the potato about ⅛ to ¼ inch wide.** (The ⅛" slices are thin, crisp, and delicious and are reminiscent of shoestring potatoes.)

3 **Stack a few of those slices, like planks, and now turn the lengthwise stack 90 degrees sideways (end to end is left to right in front of you) and cut into small sticks about ⅛ to ¼ inch wide.**

Do the same for the remaining slices. You will end up with fries about ⅛" or ¼" by 1" to 1 ½" long.

4 **Pat the potatoes very dry with paper towels.**

5 **Use enough olive oil to just cover the bottom of the skillet, but not more** (these are not deep fried potatoes.)

6 **Set your flame to medium to medium-high** (see Tip 1).

7 **When the oil is hot and just barely smoking, place all the potato pieces in a single layer in the skillet.**

Use a skillet big enough to hold all the potatoes you are cooking in as close to a single layer as possible or use more than one pan. We find one cut up potato fits a 12-inch skillet and serves two people.

8 **Sprinkle with salt and pepper to taste as they cook.**

9 **Leave the potatoes cooking on one side for a good 5 minutes.** If you move them before that they may stick to the pan.

10 **As they start to brown, flip them over with a spatula or tongs and leave them alone (another 4 to 5 minutes) until they are browned on the new side.** Note: If you cut your potatoes thin (⅛") they will cook faster.

11 **Then take a large flat spatula or tongs and turn them again to further brown.** If they are browning up a bit on each side in about 4 to 5 minutes your flame is correct. (However, as they cook longer they will naturally brown up more.)

12 **Wait another 3 to 4 minutes and turn again** (see Tip 4).

13 **When most of the potatoes are brown and/ or crisp, remove from the skillet.**

14 **Drain the potatoes on paper towels, pat to remove excess oil, and serve.**

Serve as a side or under fried or soft-boiled eggs. Delicious with a Garlic Herb Dipping Sauce (see recipe, page 72).

TIPS

1. Too high a flame, and the fries brown too fast or burn. Too low, and they won't brown properly and will be soft. Medium high on our stove seems to brown and crisp them correctly in about 15 to 20 minutes. Also, not too high a flame or you'll burn the olive oil.
2. Optional: When you first put the potatoes in, you may cover the pan for the first 3 to 5 minutes, which tends to steam the potatoes and cook them through faster. Then remove the cover and carry on per the instructions.
3. Do not constantly fiddle with the potatoes. Let them brown and crisp on a side and then flip to brown and crisp further on a new side. Near the end of the cooking you can move them around more.
4. It is all right if all of the potatoes are not evenly crisp. That gives a varied texture to the potatoes. You don't have to worry about turning every single potato perfectly each time. Just generally get the potatoes cooking and turned over when many are browned.

Mashed Potatoes

SERVES 4

Imagine if you can, where we would be without the potato, thought by many to be only a lowly tuber. In addition to the many potato recipes we have all come to love, Vodka is made from potatoes! Whether boiled, made into French fries (see recipe, page 48), sliced for Pommes Anna, or puréed into mashed potatoes, we are in its debt for the variety of dishes it offers us.

Here we give you a mashed potato recipe that is fragrant with garlic, buttery and rich with cream, and when whipped and swirled onto a platter or plate, they are ready to be crowned with a piece of fish, a slice or two of roast chicken, steak, or any variety of roasted vegetables.

To us these mashed potatoes are like eating white velvet; they are so smooth and luscious.

We have included a bonus recipe for potato cakes (see recipe, page 110) made from leftover mashed potatoes. Actually, we often double the recipe below so we are sure to have extra mashed potatoes for this purpose.

5 to 6 large baking potatoes (Idahos or Russetts)

1 cup heavy cream

10 to 12 tablespoons of unsalted butter (1 ½ sticks), at room temperature

Salt and white pepper

Garlic, 3 to 4 cloves, minced

2 tablespoons flour

1 tablespoon chopped parsley (optional)

TOOLS

- Large pot, such as a Le Creuset Dutch oven or an All-Clad stock pot that will hold the potatoes comfortably
- A colander
- A food mill, or ricer
- 3 to 4 cup heavy-bottomed saucepan
- Large bowl
- Electric handheld beater
- Wooden spoon
- Warm serving dish

Before beginning this (or any recipe containing several steps) we suggest you do a *mise en place* (literally "put in place"), the French cooking technique where you ready all of the ingredients before you actually begin the cooking process.

1 **Clean, peel and quarter potatoes and put them in a big pot with water to cover by an inch or more. Bring to a boil and cook for about 20 to 25 minutes or until tender.** Do not overcook.

2 **In the meantime, using a small saucepan, melt 6 tablespoons of butter, add the minced garlic and sauté gently until soft. Do not allow the garlic to brown.**

3 **Stir in 2 tablespoons of flour and allow it to fizzle and bubble up.** (This is an important step since it gently cooks the flour, eliminating any raw flour taste.)

4 **When the foam has subsided, slowly add 1 cup of cream, stirring constantly until slightly thickened.** Set aside, keeping it warm.

5 **When the potatoes are tender, drain them in a colander.**

6 **Put potatoes through the food mill or ricer and return them to the pot in which they were cooked over very low flame.** This will dry out any moisture left in them.

7 **To the potatoes, add 2 tablespoons of room temperature butter, salt and pepper to taste, and fold together using a big wooden paddle or wooden spoon until the butter is incorporated.**

8 **Using a handheld mixer, beat the potatoes until smooth and creamy. Do not overbeat.**

9 **Now add the garlic cream to the beaten potatoes and blend thoroughly with a wooden paddle or spoon. Correct seasoning with salt and pepper.**

10 **Turn into a warmed serving dish, put a lump of butter on top and sprinkle some chopped parsley if desired.**

TIPS

We discovered (conveniently) that preparing this several hours in advance through step 8, allows the flavors time to blend and marry even more. Set aside the potatoes and the garlic cream until serving time. Before serving, reheat the potatoes in a large pot on a diffuser and in a separate saucepan reheat the garlic cream. When both are warm, add the garlic cream to the potatoes and combine well. Correct seasoning with salt and pepper.

About Mashed Potatoes

The history of the potato is an interesting and curious one. We always thought it hailed originally from Ireland, but it actually was cultivated first in the Andes mountains of South America. Around 1536, the potato was brought to Europe by the Spanish and it was adopted by European farmers as inexpensive nutrition. Now, mashed potatoes, so revered by the French (purée de pommes de terre), is America's favorite Thanksgiving turkey accompaniment. Varieties abound, but we think our recipe interpretation of this basic French recipe wins the prize and, as it turns out, that is exactly what happened! It seems that Antoine Parmentier, a French pharmacist and physician who studied the potato, decided to hold a contest, sometime around 1789, for the best potato recipe. Not surprisingly, his own won! He mashed his and combined them with double cream, butter, salt and a bit of garlic. It was such a hit, it has endured for over two centuries—not a bad recommendation.

Potato Salad

SERVES 4

There is a myth about potato salad—that it must contain hard-boiled eggs. Where does this come from? Is it because potatoes were scarce at one time and the eggs acted as a filler? Is it to add nutrition to the dish, making it a more complete meal with some protein? We do not know the answer though we have tried to find out.

The potato salad presented here was invented as a rebellion against the hard-boiled egg-filled potato salad that almost always contains too much mayonnaise, and so you end up with a bowl of yellow goop, and not a very tasty goop at that. Now we like hard-boiled eggs. Look at the breakthrough recipe for them in this book (see recipe, page 80). They play a major role in our cooking. The addition of potato salad in our book is to have *this* potato salad free of hard-boiled eggs.

The recipe below is a first cousin to the German one, but served cold or at room temperature and without the addition of bacon grease to the dressing...but we kept the bacon, of course. Rather than the normal addition of too much vinegar, we add just a touch, of the red wine variety.

The crowning glory is the crispy, crumbled bacon, the perfect ending touch, to be mixed at the table or just before serving. The bacon eventually loses its crispness by the end of the meal since it is mixed in. However, its flavor is still very much present and we have a unique suggestion for any leftover...if there is any leftover, called Potato Salad Redux or Hash Browns (see recipe, page 110).

4 large Russet or Idaho potatoes, unpeeled washed and quartered

1 bunch scallions, green tops only, sliced

½ red onion, diced

¼ cup good mayonnaise, Hellman's (use sparingly, but to taste)

¼ cup sour cream or plain yogurt (again to taste)

½ teaspoon Dijon mustard (or to taste)

1 teaspoon red wine vinegar

Salt and pepper (to taste)

5 to 6 pieces of crisply cooked bacon, drained well and crumbled (see recipe, page 61)

TOOLS

- Large pot for cooking potatoes
- Spider or slotted spoon
- Cutting board
- Paring knife
- Large mixing bowl
- Clean dishtowel
- Small or medium-sized mixing bowl
- Rubber spatula
- Wooden spoon
- Chef's knife
- A heavy, ribbed, shallow, square, cast iron grill pan, such as Lodge

1 **Place quartered, unpeeled potatoes in a pot on the stove top with enough cold water to cover, by 2 inches.**

2 **Bring to a steady low boil over medium heat.**

3 **Cook until just knife tender, no more, about 25 to 30 minutes.**

4 While the potatoes are cooking, make the dressing. **In a small mixing bowl, combine the mayonnaise, sour cream or yogurt, mustard, red wine vinegar, and mix well with a wooden spoon and set aside.**

5 **When the potatoes are done, use a spider or slotted spoon to remove potato quarters to the cutting board.**

6 **Hold each quarter of potato in the towel to protect your hands from the heat and remove the skins with the paring knife and discard, returning the potato quarters to the cutting board.** The skins should just slide off the potato.

7 **Using your chef's knife, dice the potatoes into ½ inch pieces and place them in the bowl.**

8 **Add the diced onion and scallion tops to the potatoes.**

9 **Salt and pepper the potatoes.**

10 **Pour just enough of the dressing over them, stirring gently, to coat each piece of potato.** Take care not to break up the potato pieces. The warm potatoes will absorb the dressing giving them a creamy texture. Hold onto any extra dressing for later use (see Tips).

11 **Let cool, then cover with plastic wrap and refrigerate for several hours to develop the flavors.**

12 **About 30 minutes before serving the potato salad, place 5 to 6 pieces of bacon on a cast iron ridged skillet or ridged griddle. Place in a cold oven and turn the temperature to 400 degrees.**

13 **Cook the bacon for about 22 minutes or until just crisp. Then place on paper towels and drain well. Set aside.** For the full steps on how to prepare bacon (see recipe, page 61).

14 **While preparing the bacon, remove the potato salad from the refrigerator and allow to sit at room temperature for about 20 minutes.**

15 **Just before serving the salad, correct the seasonings for salt, pepper, and dressing. Crumble the bacon in the paper towel and sprinkle it over the top of the potato salad. Toss it all together and serve.**

TIPS

This recipe makes an ample amount of dressing, so when correcting the seasoning before serving, you can add more dressing to taste, as some will have been absorbed.

Potato Pancakes (A.K.A. Latkes)

MAKES ABOUT 25 SMALL PANCAKES

While called potato pancakes, these tasty morsels are a pancake in shape only. Not to be confused with our potato cakes (see recipe, page 110) made from left over mashed potatoes. These are a family favorite comfort food and are delicious anytime of the year.

Served alone or as a side to any meat dish with which you would serve potatoes, do not make your guests choose between the traditional accompaniments of sour cream *or* applesauce as most restaurants do. Serve the potato pancakes with both!

5 large Idaho or Russet potatoes

2 eggs

⅛ teaspoon baking powder

1 ½ teaspoons salt

2 tablespoons flour

1 small onion, grated (or to taste)

Dash of pepper

¼ teaspoon nutmeg, grated (or to taste)

Grapeseed or Peanut oil for frying

TOOLS

- Box grater
- Large bowl
- Potato peeler
- Clean dishtowel
- 12 to 14-inch stainless steel skillet or a large electric skillet
- Baking sheet lined with paper towels

1 **Pre-heat oven to 200 degrees.**

2 **Peel potatoes, grate them on a box grater or the grater attachment of your food processor.**

3 **Drain very well by squeezing as much moisture as possible out of the grated potatoes by twisting them in a clean dish towel. Empty them into a large bowl.**

4 **In a separate bowl, beat eggs well.**

5 **Mix the eggs in with the shredded potatoes, the baking powder, salt, pepper, flour, onion, and nutmeg.**

6 **Heat about a ¼ inch of peanut or grapeseed oil and a tablespoon of butter in a skillet.** The oil should be hot, but not smoking.

7 **Drop about 2 tablespoons of the potato mixture into the hot oil/butter, making a pancake about 2 to 3 inches in diameter.** This allows you to cook several at a time.

8 **Brown the pancakes well on both sides, about 5 minutes per side.**

9 **Drain on a paper towel-lined sheet pan.**

Note: You may make the pancakes larger in diameter or thicker, depending on your preference and what else you are serving with them. The smaller version in this recipe serves as a side dish accompanying a full meal and allows you to make 5 to 7 at a time.

10 **Keep warm in a 200 degree oven or serve immediately.**

Serve with Applesauce (see recipe, page 62) and sour cream.

ON THE SIDE

Training is everything. The peach was once a bitter almond; Cauliflower is nothing but cabbage with a college education.

— MARK TWAIN

Pan-Fried Toast

SERVES 1 SLICE PER PERSON

Our research shows that in 1905, two Chicago inventors discovered an alloy that permitted a fire-safe toaster to be manufactured. Today, 88% of American households have a toaster. We are part of the 12% that do not have a toaster due to the delicious alternative recipe we present to you here.

Do not underestimate how delicious, useful and yes, even heavenly, properly made toast can be.

Yes, it is a quick breakfast with a bit of butter and jam smeared on top. True, it is a fast food of sorts when peanut butter or a slice of melted cheese is all you have around. But we think that toast, albeit pan-fried toast, is one of the great platforms for excellent cuisine.

We have not used a toaster in years because of the superior method described in our recipe. The resulting toast is absolutely delicious and can form the base for so many different foods; as an accompaniment to eggs, including Egg-In-The Bowl (see recipe, page 74), or as croutons in soup. Even further, pan-fried toast is perfect as the stage for a poached egg topped with sautéed mushrooms, or cut into rounds or shaped into squares or narrow rectangles as a platform for hors d'oeuvres, as the deck for hamburgers or lamb burgers, and as a simple delight with good butter or preserves.

The key to this recipe is very good quality bread and the technique described below.

A good loaf of bread, such as Italian artisan bread, other bakery-fresh or homemade bread (see Tip 3)

Olive Oil

Butter (optional)

Salt (optional)

Garlic (optional) slices or crushed

TOOLS

- Skillet, either a good cast iron pan, steel mineral pan (de Buyer), or a stainless steel pan (All-Clad), big enough not to crowd the slices.

1 **Take a slice of bread about ¼ to ½ inch thick.** The thicker the slice, the softer the inside will be. Optionally, at this point you can sprinkle a little salt on one side of the bread.

2 **Put olive oil in the skillet. Turn the flame to medium or to medium-high.** Optionally, add a tablespoon of butter to the olive oil. Use enough olive oil to just cover half the bottom of the pan. You can always add more if the bread absorbs it all (see Tip 1).

3 **When the oil is getting hot, but not smoking, add the bread and sauté, turning it several times until is browned and crisp on both sides.** Add more olive oil as needed to keep the pan moist and the toast crisping.

4 **When crisp and crusted on each side, serve the bread hot.**

TIPS

1. It is the interaction between the oil and the bread that creates a nice crust. If the bread soaks up the oil, add more oil to facilitate this interaction.
2. For a healthier, different, denser taste, we often use Low Sodium Ezekiel bread and keep it frozen in the freezer. When we need a slice we cut it off and either bring it to room temperature or just fry it frozen as it soon thaws. Frozen bread avoids the problem of bread going stale after a few days.
3. When using good artisan bread, we prefer unsliced bread, so we can determine the thickness or thinness of the slices. And we believe unsliced bread keeps fresher longer. The thicker the slice, the softer and less done it will be inside while the outside is crisp. Thicker slices or even thick end cuts off a fine artisan bread are often a delicious variation.
4. Optional: as a savory taste supplement, add some sliced or crushed garlic to the oil once the bread has been cooking. The garlic will infuse the oil and bread with its flavor. Do this step part way through the cooking, as garlic burns easily.

Creamed Spinach

SERVES 4

The Standard Club in Chicago, a private club with elegant food, serves creamed spinach fit for a king. Many restaurant creamed spinach recipes are so processed the end result is more like unappetizing baby food. Some are too chunky with a poor mouth feel, and others are watery and salty.

The following recipe is based on what the Standard Club serves, redolent with nutmeg and garlic and just a touch of cream.

The secret to this dish is to squeeze every drop of moisture out of the cooked spinach, followed by a very fine chop with a good, sharp chef's knife. We found that chopping the spinach very, very finely not only ensures no stringy fibers remain, but gives the final result a wonderfully smooth texture.

Face it, what tastes better accompanying a meat entrée and mashed potatoes than fragrant creamed spinach? Not much.

This is a recipe that reminds us of home, the holidays, warm and inviting times in our life.

Make it so for you, as well.

---

3 to 4 bags of fresh spinach. (Although you can use frozen spinach, fresh is superior in this recipe)

1 medium yellow onion, finely diced

1 small garlic clove, finely chopped

2 tablespoons butter

¾ cup heavy whipping cream

Kosher salt to taste

Freshly ground white pepper, to taste

1 teaspoon freshly grated nutmeg or to taste

TOOLS

- Colander
- Clean cotton dish towel
- Chef's knife, 10-inch or better 12-inch
- 12-inch nonstick or enameled skillet
- Wooden or silicone spatula

1 **Preferably using fresh spinach, steam it until it is just wilted.** If using frozen spinach and it is already cooked, proceed to step 2 after thawing it.

2 **Drain as much water as possible out of the spinach by pressing it with a big spoon in a colander.**

3 **Then place the damp spinach into a clean dishtowel and squeeze the remaining water out of it until it is very dry.**

4 **Chop the spinach very, very finely with a long, sharp knife and when you think you have done so, do it again.** We like to use a very long 12-inch knife as it reaches over the mound of spinach nicely when chopping it.

5 **In a heavy, non-reactive skillet** (we use a large nonstick skillet with straight sides), **melt the butter over medium heat.**

6 **Add the finely chopped onion and sauté until onion is translucent, but not browned.**

7 **Add garlic and sauté briefly until fragrant.**

8 **Add chopped, squeezed spinach to the pan and sauté until warmed through.**

9 **Stir gently with wooden or heatproof silicone spatula, while adding heavy cream slowly to the pan and heat through thoroughly blending for about 10 minutes.** Add just enough cream so the spinach is wet but not swimming and has the consistency of soft oatmeal. The amount of cream added is a matter of taste but critical (we use very little cream which gives the dish a bright green and slightly enriched taste).

10 As the spinach cooks, season to taste with salt, pepper and nutmeg. Combine well. Taste and adjust as needed.

11 Continue cooking slowly until very warm and a thick, somewhat creamy texture is achieved.

TIPS

1. We discovered (conveniently) that preparing this several hours in advance and keeping it warm in a pan on a diffuser or in an electric skillet allows the flavors time to blend and marry even more. Just before serving reheat to very warm or hot and refresh with a little more cream and butter as needed to serve it moist.
2. Even more conveniently, prepare the spinach as above. Let it cool down and refrigerate over night in an airtight container or bag. When ready to serve the next day, or much later that same day, reheat it adding a little cream and butter to remoisten and refresh. Add more salt and pepper as needed. Delicious.

Applesauce

SERVES 4

This is the freshest, healthiest applesauce you have probably ever tasted; and more to the point, it is delicious.

What we often think of as a sweet and bland cooked fruit, easy for young children to eat or as an easily digested food, we have transformed into a gourmet dish to accompany meat entrées, such as our Baby Back Ribs—Chicago Style (see recipe, page 38). It has a luscious mouth feel and gives real balance and contrasting texture to very rich meats. Unlike other applesauce recipes, it requires no cooking at all.

The texture, the color, and the flavor make for an unusual and delectable apple purée that will leave your guests wondering how you achieved it.

8 organic, unpeeled, red delicious apples (figure two apples per person)

1 teaspoon cinnamon

2 to 3 tablespoons honey or to taste (we prefer raw Clover honey)

TOOLS

- Large wooden or silicon spoon
- Sharp knife
- Blender, Vitamix or comparable professional blender

1 **Clean, core, quarter, and slice apples. Do not peel.**

2 **Place cut up apples in a very high quality blender such as a Vitamix. Fill to near the top of the container, making it easier to push the apples down once blending begins.**

3 **Add the cinnamon and honey.** Take care to not overdo the seasoning and sweetness as the applesauce will not be balanced.

4 **Using the Vitamix plunger, blend all ingredients for 60 seconds or more until very smooth with absolutely no visible particles** (see Tip 2). If using another blender, turn to high and blend until very smooth.

5 **Add more apples as needed to the blender mixture and blend as above** (if not enough room, blend another batch of apples after pouring off the blended sauce).

6 **Taste to make sure the sauce is smoother than baby food. Adjust seasoning as needed.**

7 **Pour into glass jars and refrigerate overnight to allow flavors to marry. It is clearly much better tasting the next day.**

Note: If using more than 8 to 10 apples, you will need to work in batches.

Serve with ribs or other rich meat dishes.

Optional: Also perfect for that teething baby.

TIPS

1. One of the secrets to the recipe is thorough blending, which somehow releases flavor into the sauce. The sauce will even get a little warm during this lengthy blending.
2. If using a Vitamix, a tamper is provided to help push down and mix the raw apples as they are blending. Otherwise, the apples will ride on the top of the blades. We suggest pushing down at each corner of the blender with the plunger.

Grilled Bacon

SERVES 2 SLICES PER PERSON

Who doesn't know how to cook bacon? Is it as easy as people think? It wasn't for us until we discovered a method that assures that this delectable pork treat is maximized.

Skillet frying produces a fat-laden bacon that tends to curl, wrinkle, and is oily, in our view. Microwaving can dry bacon out and make the meat parts tough.

We discovered that bacon has a great taste when cooked in a ridged cast iron grill pan with ¾" high sides all around. Those ridges allow the fat to drip down and away from the bacon. We use a Lodge 12-inch cast iron square grill pan with a convenient handle. It produces great results.

Regardless of method, you must begin with the finest quality bacon you can find. We prefer natural organic, artisan bacon, thick sliced at our local butcher shop.

4 to 6 slices of bacon (Beeler's or your favorite) or however many your grill pan will hold without over-crowding

TOOLS

- A heavy, ribbed, shallow, square, cast iron grill pan (we use a Lodge, 12-inch Square Grill Pan) with handle or even a ribbed cast iron skillet. In a pinch one can use a rimmed baking sheet with an inserted cooling rack/grid upon which one places the bacon so the fat runs down into the baking sheet
- Tongs
- Paper towels

1 **Allow the bacon to come to room temperature, 20 to 30 minutes.**

2 **Place the bacon slices on the ribbed grill pan with about ¼ inch between slices.**

3 **Place into the middle of a cold oven.**

4 **Close door and set oven to 400 degrees.**

5 **Set your timer for 18 to 22 minutes** (see Tip 1).

6 **After about 16 minutes check the bacon to see how it is coming. Ovens will vary the speed of cooking as will the thickness of the bacon.**

7 **When the bacon is done to your liking, remove with tongs to paper towels to drain.**

Serve immediately.

TIPS

1. If you like your bacon very crisp you'll be closer to 20 minutes or more. If you prefer your bacon less crisp, you'll be closer to 18 minutes or even less. Remember, ovens vary in temperature as does the thickness of the bacon. Watch the cooking time closely after 16 minutes or so until you know how long to cook it in the future, when you can set your timer exactly.
2. We use a Lodge, Pro-Logic 12-inch Grill Pan for bacon. It has a handle making it easy to lift, it has ridges that keep the bacon out of the grease, and it is cast iron, which is conducive to high heat. It is also suitable for many other cooking chores in the kitchen, especially when you want grill marks on meat.

Coleslaw

SERVES 4 TO 6

Coleslaw is one of those great American side dishes that seems to accompany almost everything we eat in restaurants. Diners put it in little paper, fluted cups on the side of the plate to accompany a sandwich. Rib joints put it in an even smaller paper cup, the size of a thimble and shove it on the plate between the ribs and something else. Have you noticed that it is the same coleslaw and is invariably chopped very finely, has two or three flecks of carrot in it, and is loaded with so much mayonnaise that it is nearly liquid?

We present you with a coleslaw that has backbone, that is compatible with even the spiciest foods, is highly flavorful, but is a cooling accompaniment to our savory Baby Back Ribs—Chicago Style or Braised Short Ribs (see recipes, page 38 and 44).

This coleslaw has a unique texture and taste that is due to the way the cabbage is cored and sliced (see Tips). It is not a sloppy slaw, even though it has a mayonnaise-based dressing. It has body and subtle flavors; ginger, lemon zest, and celery seed: small amounts of each to give only a hint of their flavor; just enough to make your guests say, "What am I tasting here that is so different and refreshing?"

This slaw is a wonderful complement to our Applesauce (see recipe, page 60) and is delicious on top of a Memphis Pulled Pork Sandwich (see recipe, page 39).

1 head of organic green cabbage, outer leaves removed

1 small carrot, roughly grated

2 to 3 tablespoons red onion, finely minced

1 teaspoon lemon zest, or to taste

Green tops of a small bunch of scallions, about 2 tablespoons, chopped roughly

5 tablespoons mayonnaise or to taste

2 to 3 tablespoons of sour cream

1 tablespoon red wine vinegar

1 teaspoon green peppercorn mustard

1 teaspoon ginger root, very finely chopped or grated

¼ teaspoon celery seed

scant ½ teaspoon salt
Caution: salt will leach water from cabbage, so use sparingly to avoid diluting the dressing and producing a "sloppy" coleslaw

½ teaspoon freshly ground pepper

TOOLS

- Sharp chef's knife
- Box grater
- Large glass bowl
- Smaller mixing bowl
- Measuring spoons
- Microplane

1 **Orient the cabbage so the stub (flat) end of the core is resting downward on the cutting board.** This gives both stability and makes cutting safer and easier.

2 **Using a very sharp knife, cut the cabbage in two, splitting the core down the center** (see illustration 1).

3 **Turn each half on its flat side, and cut in half, again through the length of core.** This creates four wedges total (see illustration 2).

4 **Remove the hard, white center core of each wedge using a sharp knife.** (Not shown in illustrations.)

5 **Now turn the four wedges so that the long side of the wedge is parallel to you. Cut into inch slices** (see illustration 3).

6 **Then turn the wedge so it is perpendicular to you (and the slices are parallel to you) and cut into ½" to 1" bite-sized chunks** (see illustration 4).

7 **Place all of the cut cabbage into a large bowl.**

8 **Using the largest openings of a box grater, grate the carrot into chips or bits and add it to the bowl.**

9 **Add the red onion (finely minced) the chopped scallion tops, and celery seed. Mix well.** (We use our hands, "impeccably clean", of course, to quote Julia Child and Sara Moulton).

10 **For the dressing: in a separate smaller bowl, mix together the mayonnaise, sour cream, red wine vinegar, very finely chopped ginger root, lemon zest, and mustard.** We use a microplane for the lemon zest.

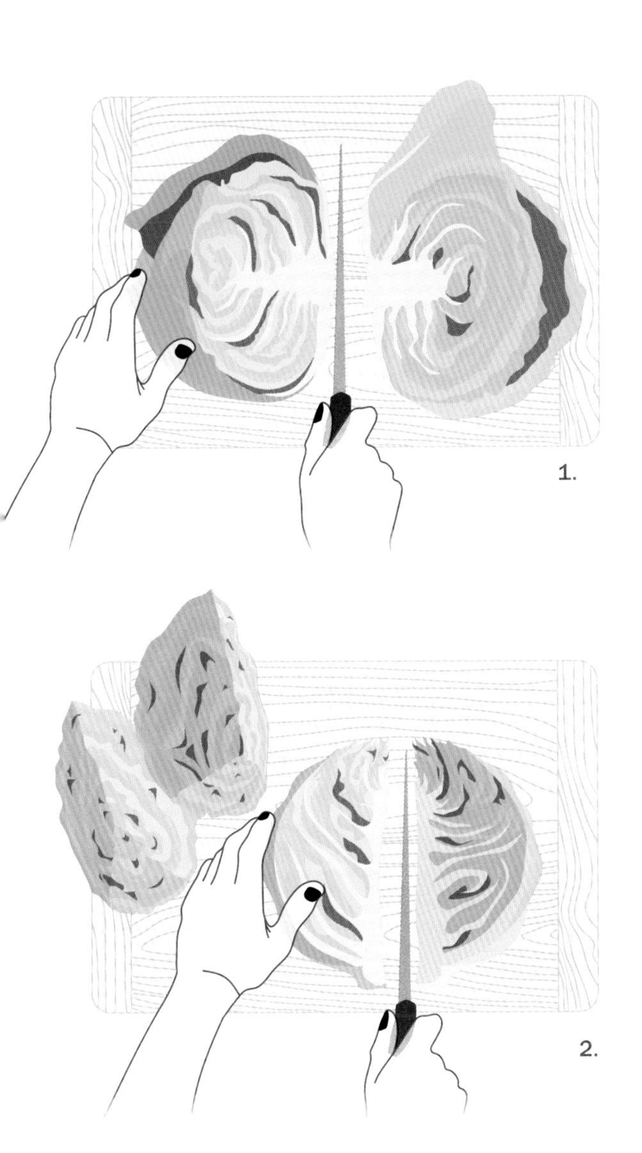

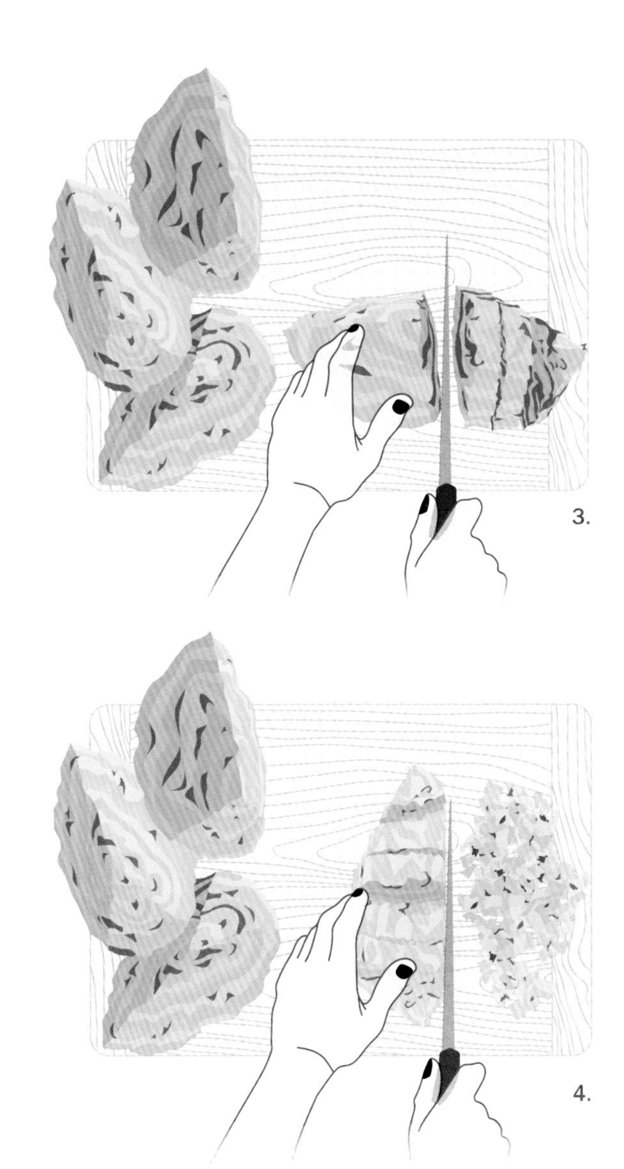

11 **Add just enough of the dressing to the cabbage mixture to coat all of the ingredients. Reserve the remainder.**

12 **Place the slaw in glass jars and refrigerate for several hours or better, overnight.** It is vital that the flavors be allowed to marry.

Before serving, turn the jar of slaw upside down to remix the dressing, which tends to settle overnight. If it appears to have collected too much liquid, then drain some of it out of the jar. Then correct seasoning as needed and stir well before serving. If slaw seems dry, add the reserved dressing.

Coleslaw *continued*

TIPS

The cutting of the cabbage is important to the final result. If you shred the cabbage by cutting it into thin, string-like slices, the end result will be a very wet, sloppy coleslaw. If you cut it as directed above, the result will be a slaw with body and the bite-sized pieces will support the dressing, rather than absorb it.

About Coleslaw

Coleslaw, primarily a cold cabbage salad, has its origins in Germany, Poland, and the Netherlands. The Italians, too have a version of this favorite, called Insalata Capricciosa, or roughly translated "capricious salad."

Pickled, it can last for weeks in the refrigerator as the Germans do with their Krautsalad.

It was the Dutch who actually brought it to the New World. Its name means "kool salad" or cabbage salad, but in the 19th century, the term "cold slaw" was also used. Perhaps that is what gave American cooks the idea to serve it with spicy dishes.

In the US, it is traditional picnic fare to combine mayonnaise or buttermilk and often mustard. If it is being served as "barbecue slaw" or red slaw, it has the addition of ketchup and vinegar in lieu of mayonnaise or buttermilk. Coleslaw is an essential accompaniment to southern variations of barbecue.

Classic Onion Rings

SERVES 2

Is there any side dish that is a better, more tempting accompaniment to steak, hamburger, fish, or as a stand-by-itself snack, than onion rings? It is one of our favorites and this recipe is so easy to make and so delicious, it should probably be illegal! Carol has served these for years and often, all other food is ignored while every crumb of these onion rings is devoured.

Served alone, with one of our dipping sauces (recipes page 72, 108), or with artisan ketchup, this is a treat that your family and friends will love and won't believe they can make at home. As a matter of fact, very often it is the only item of the meal that they seem to remember for years to come!

1 large yellow onion

Peanut or Grapeseed oil to come up a full inch in your pan

12 oz. or 1 ½ cups beer

1 ½ cup All-Purpose flour

Salt to taste

Optional: Ketchup

TOOLS

- Large skillet, such as a 12-inch cast iron, 12-inch stainless steel, or electric stainless steel skillet
- Thermometer (for use in hot oil)
- Large bowl
- Whisk
- Tongs
- Paper towel-lined baking sheet(s)

TIPS

As an alternative, the batter is equally appropriate for veggies, such as mushrooms, eggplant, sweet potatoes, green beans, or whatever fish or seafood you prefer, such as shrimp, scallops, or other firm white fish cut into bite-sized pieces. Proceed as you would using an onion, cooking longer where appropriate.

1 **In a large bowl, use a whisk to mix the flour and beer together until smooth.** The beer can be cold, at room temperature, flat or newly opened. It matters not. The result will be equally wonderful.

2 **Cover the bowl with plastic wrap and allow to stand at room temperature for two hours.** This allows the gluten in the flour to develop. This is what gives the finished onion ring or vegetable, or piece of fish its crispy texture.

3 **Pre-heat oven to 200 degrees.**

4 **Cut onion into slices about ¼ of an inch thick.** To create onion rings, cut off the stem end and root end of the onion. Peel off the skin or outer layer. Cut ¼" slices in the same direction as you did to cut off the root and stem. Break up the slices gently so you end up with individual rings.

5 **Heat oil until it reaches a temperature of 350 to 375 degrees.**

6 **While the oil is heating, put several onion rings into the batter and stir until well-coated.**

7 **When the oil reaches 350 to 375 degrees, using tongs, begin putting onions, ring by ring, into the oil, being careful not to splash yourself.** Each onion ring should float in the hot oil by itself. Do not leave the stove. They cook very quickly. Turn them once when the desired color is achieved.

8 **As each ring is cooked, carefully remove it one by one to the towel-lined baking sheet and repeat with remaining onions.** If making quite a few or if the remainder of your dinner (if you are having anything else) is not yet ready, you will want to keep them warm in the oven, at 200 degrees.

9 **Salt to taste.**

Serve with dipping sauces such as Garlic Herb Dipping Sauce (see recipe, page 72) or if desired, a good quality artisan ketchup.

Seared Asparagus

SERVES 5 TO 7 SPEARS PER PERSON

People usually boil or steam asparagus. These methods are fine and we sometimes use them when serving asparagus with our Chicago Cream Sauce (see recipe, page 38). But, we prefer to pan sear asparagus in olive oil, often with garlic. The color will be bright, but additionally, you will get marks that show how the vegetable has caramelized and that means greater flavor. This simple and healthy method of cooking asparagus makes them remarkably sweet and still crisp.

This very same recipe works well with vegetables such as broccoli, carrots, onions, parsnips or any firm veggie of your choice.

1 pound of the freshest asparagus

Olive oil

Kosher salt

Black pepper

Optional: garlic (sliced or chopped. The thinner it is sliced, the more flavor will infuse)

TOOLS

- 12-inch or 14-inch skillet, mineral steel (such as de Buyer), cast iron (such as a Lodge), or stainless steel (such as an All-Clad)
- Vegetable peeler
- Tongs or spatula
- Paper towels

1 **Put the olive oil in the pan and heat until it is hot.**

2 **In the meantime, cut about ½″ of the woody ends off the asparagus.**

3 **If the asparagus is thick and large, peel away the outer skin of the bottom half of the stalk.** If young and thin, this step is not necessary.

4 **When the oil is smoking slightly, add the asparagus to the skillet. Season with salt and pepper.**

5 **Sear the asparagus on the first side leaving it alone until browned and bright green.**

6 **Turn the asparagus with the tongs or spatula onto the uncooked side.**

7 **If using garlic add it soon after turning the asparagus over and move it around in the oil to spread its flavor.** If you add the garlic before this point you risk burning it.

8 **Cook until the asparagus is browned on each side.** Do not overcook. You want the asparagus firm to the touch, not the least bit mushy. Drain on paper towels.

Serve as a side vegetable with any of our meat dishes or with two fried or soft-boiled eggs placed on top, or with several spoonfuls of Chicago Cream Sauce (see recipe, page 38).

TIPS

1. Learn to use the right pan or skillet for the right job. In this case you want a nice dark sear on the asparagus and that calls for a metal or cast iron pan of some kind, not a nonstick pan which one uses for low and moderate cooking, such as with eggs. Metal pans are excellent for high heat and searing. Our personal favorite for asparagus is the large 14-inch de Buyer mineral steel pan. It affords lots of room for the long pieces of asparagus and gives them a beautiful sear and flavor.
2. Do not overcrowd the pan. If the asparagus are too close or piled on top of each other, they will steam rather than fry and as a result, they will not cook evenly.

SAUCES

If you are afraid of butter, use cream.

— JULIA CHILD

Chicago Cream Sauce

MAKES ABOUT 2 CUPS

We created this irresistible sauce as a practical alternative to the infamously finicky hollandaise. We actually prefer its taste and it is healthier to boot. More to the point, we wanted an all-purpose sauce that stores well and that could be used on a variety of foods.

The sauce can be prepared up to two days in advance (it is better after many hours as it marries up) and stored in a glass jar. It is delicious served over asparagus, broccoli, sautéed mushrooms, or other vegetables, eggs, steak, salmon, or other fish, and with cold leftover meats. And it can be spiced up with greater amounts of cayenne (to contrast against the creamy texture of the sauce or no cayenne for those who like a more neutral taste), pepper, or mustard, such as when served with steak (remember steak au poivre?). As is common with many sauces, one can add depth and viscosity to the basic recipe by the addition of butter at the end.

Just as we were writing this, we put two gently fried eggs over Seared Asparagus (see recipe, page 65) topped with Chicago Cream Sauce—a simple, heavenly dinner.

In making the sauce, give yourself enough time (an hour or more) to reduce the sauce per the instructions.

3 cups vegetable broth

3 tarragon sprigs (leaves only), finely minced (or 1 tablespoon of dried tarragon)

3 chervil sprigs, finely minced or 1 tablespoon dry minced chervil (if not available in your area you can use parsley as a substitute)

¾ teaspoon chives

2 small shallots, finely minced

1 teaspoon of Dijon mustard

¼ cup of dry white wine

1 tablespoon white wine vinegar

1 teaspoon of salt

⅛ teaspoon of freshly ground pepper

⅛ teaspoon of cayenne pepper (or to taste)

1 cup cream

2 teaspoons cornstarch

1 tablespoon lemon juice, strained

1 to 2 tablespoon chilled butter (optional)

TOOLS

- Saucier or normal saucepan, preferably with a large surface area. We prefer the wide deep sauté pan made by Le Creuset (which serves as a large saucier) with its enamel finish and large, skillet-like surface area, but any good high quality saucier or saucepan will do, such as All-Clad. In this case, a wider pan is beneficial for reducing the sauce, but not essential. (A saucier has gently sloping sides, allowing effective whisking of the sauce.)
- Wooden paddle (we use those made by Michael Ruhlman) or a heatproof silicone spatula both of which are better for scraping the bottom and sides of a pan
- Whisk (rubber or silicone coated if whisking in an enameled or nonstick saucier or saucepan)
- Optional: diffuser
- Glass storage jars

1 **For the first 11 ingredients, do your *mise en place*** (see Tip 1).

2 **In the saucepan, combine vegetable broth, tarragon, chervil, chives, shallots, mustard, wine, white wine vinegar, salt, pepper, and cayenne pepper.**

3 **Simmer the contents uncovered over medium heat.** Use a diffuser if possible for more even simmering. You should observe a constant, small, and low bubbling of the sauce. Do not turn the heat up too high or the sauce will cook off too quickly.

4 **Stirring occasionally, reduce the sauce to 1 ½ to 1 cup.** The sauce will thicken as it reduces. This step develops and concentrates flavor and is very important, but do not reduce beyond 1 cup. This will take about one hour.

5 **In a separate bowl, slowly whisk the cream into the cornstarch until fully dissolved.** You can use a large measuring cup to hold the cream and cornstarch which makes combining the mixture easier in the next step.

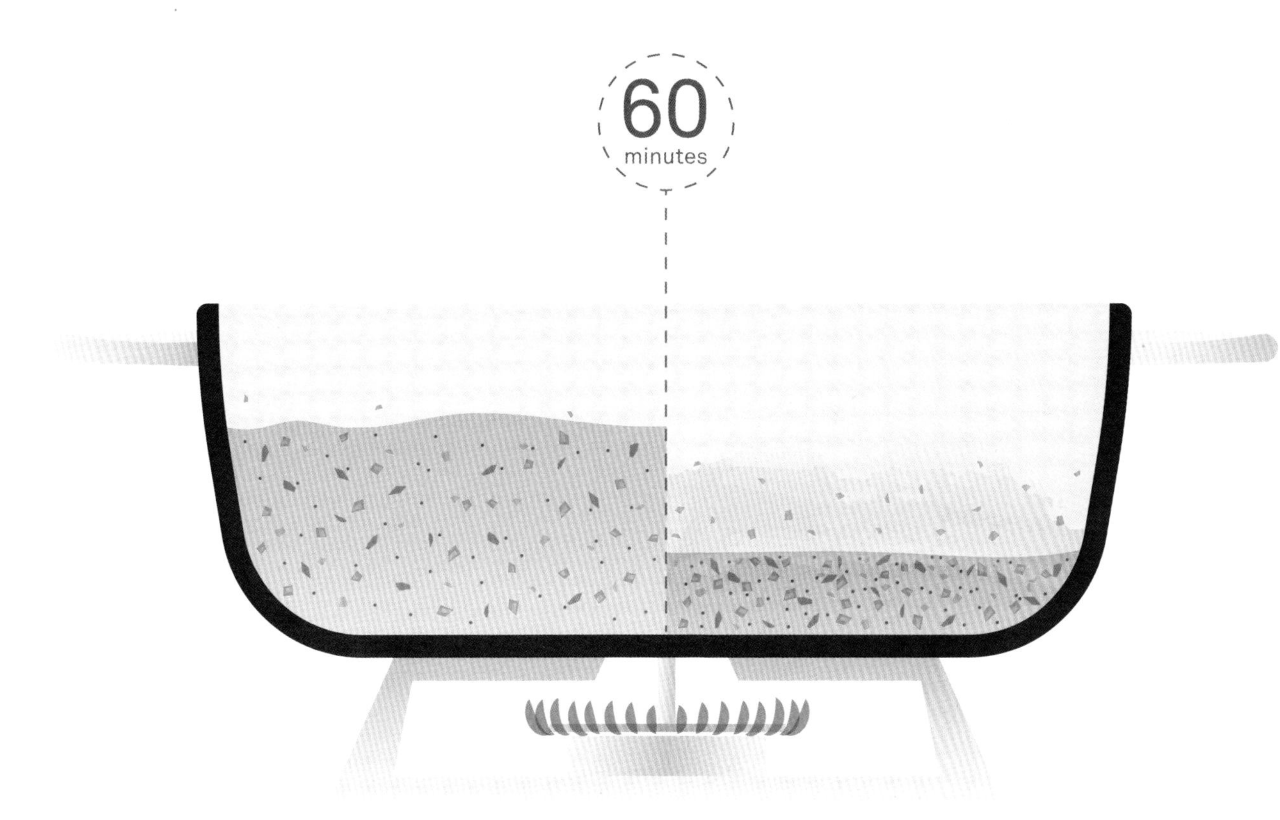

6 **Slowly whisk the cream and cornstarch mixture into the reduced sauce.**

7 **Continue to cook the sauce at slightly more than a simmer until it is further thickened** You want the cornstarch to thoroughly cook, about 5 to 10 minutes more. **Stir often and do not allow it to boil. Season with salt and pepper to taste.** The sauce should be the consistency of a typical hollandaise or béarnaise sauce, which will coat the back of a wooden spoon or paddle when lifted from the saucepan (see Tip 2).

8 **Remove from heat and stir in the lemon juice.**

9 **Allow the sauce to cool if not serving immediately.**

10 **Store in a glass jar with an airtight lid for several hours or overnight.**

The sauce will marry up as it rests and the developed taste is even better than when first made.

TIPS

1. *Mise en place* is a French term used by chefs to refer to the preparation of all ingredients before beginning any recipe. Each ingredient is placed in its own prep bowl and assembled on a cutting board or suitable surface. As you follow the recipe directions, each ingredient has been measured and gathered in one place, making your cooking more accurate and more efficient. If you get in the habit of doing the *mise en place* each time you cook, you will see its advantage.
2. Optionally: for an even thicker, richer sauce, add 1 or 2 tablespoons of chilled butter to the sauce near the end of cooking and combine well with a wooden paddle. Let the sauce thicken for a few more minutes before taking off the stove.

Sweet and Sour Barbecue Sauce

MAKES ABOUT 3 CUPS

A basic, yet sophisticated tasting barbecue sauce, this is highly seasoned and thick, making a great sauce or glaze for meat.

This is an unusual recipe in that the majority of the process is what we call *mise en place*, the French cooking technique that calls for all of the ingredients in a recipe to be measured and assembled before beginning the cooking. While the vinegars are reducing, we highly recommend carrying out the *mise en place* as it will be a much easier recipe to do.

The sauce is fabulous with braised short ribs (see recipe, page 44), chicken, pork, or any meat that is enhanced with barbecue sauce.

¾ cup balsamic vinegar, or to taste

¼ cup orange vinegar

½ red onion, diced

7 cloves of garlic, minced

2 tablespoons orange juice

1 cup Heinz ketchup

6 ounces beer

¼ cup honey

3 tablespoons grainy mustard

1 tablespoon molasses

1 tablespoon hoisin sauce (we prefer Koon Chun)

1 ½ teaspoon Worcestershire sauce

½ teaspoon cayenne, or to taste

3 grinds of black pepper

1 teaspoon dried thyme

1 tablespoon dry sherry

¼ cup dark brown sugar, or to taste

2 teaspoons salt

½ cup water

TOOLS

- Le Creuset sauté pan with a large surface area (12 inches or more in diameter). We prefer the wide deep sauté pan made by Le Creuset with its enamel finish and large, skillet-like surface area, but any good high quality saucier or saucepan will do, such as All-Clad. In this case, a larger pan is beneficial for reducing the sauce, but not essential. (A saucier has sloping sides, allowing effective whisking of the sauce)
- A wooden paddle (we use those made by Michael Ruhlman) or a heatproof silicone spatula both of which are better for scraping the bottom and sides of a pan (see Tip 2)
- Glass storage jars

1 **Place the balsamic and orange vinegars in a large non-reactive skillet or saucepan, place on a diffuser if possible, and bring to a gentle boil over medium heat.**

2 **Then reduce the flame a bit and cook at a medium simmer until it is reduced by a third, which should take about 30 to 40 minutes.** *Do this step in a well-ventilated room as the fumes from the vinegars are at first quite strong.*

3 **While the vinegars reduce, prepare all of the remaining ingredients which is called *mise en place*** (see Tip 1).

4 **When the vinegars are reduced, add all of the remaining ingredients along with ½ cup water.** Stir to combine well with a wooden paddle, scraping the bottom of the pan well.

5 **Bring back to a low boil, then reduce the heat to medium low or so, and simmer until thick, 30 to 40 minutes.**

6 **If the sauce becomes too thick, add a little water.**

7 Adjust to taste by adding more vinegar, or salt and pepper.

8 When complete, pour into glass jars and cool before refrigerating overnight to allow the flavors to marry.

**Note:* *A doubled version of this sauce is contained within our Braised Short Ribs (see recipe, page 44). Should you love it as much as we do, we suggest doubling the recipe as it is written there and storing it in the refrigerator for up to a week.*

TIPS

1. *Mise en place* is a French term used by chefs to refer to the preparation of all ingredients before beginning any recipe. Each ingredient is placed in its own prep bowl and assembled on a cutting board or suitable surface. As you follow the recipe directions, each ingredient has been measured and gathered in one place, making your cooking more accurate and more efficient. If you get in the habit of doing the *mise en place* each time you cook, you will see its advantage.
2. Through trial and error we found a flat wooden paddle or silicone spatula works much better than a traditional wooden spoon for stirring sauces and scrambled eggs. The flat surface scrapes up the ingredients much more efficiently. We get our wooden paddles from Michael Ruhlman's website. Silicone spatulas are widely available.
3. When doing any long simmering on the stovetop, we find a diffuser essential or even for cooking at low temperatures such as eggs. A diffuser evens out the heat of the gas flame and gives more precise control. You can keep the food at a steady low simmer, spreading the heat evenly throughout the pan or skillet. We use an artisan copper diffuser (made by Bella) that works perfectly, as copper is an excellent conductor of heat.

Garlic Herb Dipping Sauce

MAKES ABOUT 1 CUP

This simple little sauce is perfect for dipping French Fries or to accompany hard-boiled eggs, cold fish, or cold meats. It is a sort of mock aïoli, the French sauce originated in Provence and served along side toasty French bread slices or croutons in Bouillabaisse, the famous fish stew.

It is a delicious accompaniment to many dishes and quickly put together.

½ cup of (good quality) mayonnaise, we use Hellman's

1 large clove of garlic, finely minced

1 teaspoon Dijon-type mustard

1 teaspoon dried thyme

1 or 2 twists of fresh black pepper

TOOLS

- Medium sized bowl
- Whisk or spoon

1. **Mix all of the ingredients in a bowl and blend thoroughly.**
2. **Cover with plastic wrap and refrigerate for at least a few hours or more to allow the flavors to develop.**
3. **Give it a quick stir before serving and, of course, taste and correct seasoning.**

Note: If tightly stored, it will last several days in the refrigerator.

About Aïoli

This sauce originated in Provence in Southern France. Prepared as Julia Child would have us do, it traditionally calls for the use of a mortar and pestle (to mash garlic and bread into a paste), an egg yolk, day old bread, 4 to 8 cloves of garlic, milk, and fish stock. It is not the simple sauce that we present to you here.

Aïoli is absolutely delicious served with boiled fish, bourride and bouillabaisse, (both French Provencal fish soups or stews), boiled potatoes, green beans, and hard-boiled eggs. It is fabulous with sautéed sweet potatoes, crab claws, tilapia, grilled asparagus, lamb burgers or as a dipping sauce for French fries, cooked shrimp, cold roasted vegetables, cold salmon, or cold chicken.

We think that while the classic cook will say we are cheating, and we would agree, there is something to say for a 3 to 5 minute sauce that is divine, in contrast to spending the afternoon in the kitchen laboring.

EGGS

Probably one of the most private things in the world is an egg before it is broken.

— MFK FISHER

Egg-In-The-Bowl

SERVES 1 OR 2 EGGS PER PERSON

This is Jonathan's favorite breakfast, created and eaten by him at a very early age. In fact, it is the first dish he composed. Without knowing the term "comfort food," his concept was just that. Even today, when in the mood for simple comfort food, we make Egg-In-The-Bowl for lunch or dinner. It saves time and is, for us, as good as any food.

The dish consists simply of eggs and high quality toast broken up and mixed together in a bowl. The eggs can be either soft-boiled, poached, gently (low flame) fried sunny side up, or over very easy. However, the yolks must run free so they are absorbed by the broken up pieces of toast.

This is one of the simplest dishes there is and is absolutely delicious and satisfying.

1 or 2 eggs per person

Salt and pepper

Bread for toast (see Tips)

TOOLS

- Pan to cook the eggs whatever style is chosen
- 1 serving bowl per person to hold eggs and toast
- Fork, spoon and knife

1 **Cook the eggs by frying, poaching, or steaming, Season to taste.** (See The Fried Egg recipe, page 78 and see Soft-Boiled Eggs recipe, page 81 for how to steam eggs.)

2 **As the eggs are cooking, make the toast. Our favorite method is to put olive oil (and a little butter and garlic if you wish) in a mineral metal pan, iron skillet or stainless steel pan, and pan fry the bread on each side under medium high heat.** You can add some salt to one side of the bread before frying it. Bread fried in this manner is a simple culinary delight (see recipe, page 56).

3 **Cut or break the pan-fried toast into bite-sized or smaller pieces. Put them in the bowl.**

4 **Then place the cooked eggs in with the bread, cutting and mixing them up so the yellow and white thoroughly blend in with the pieces of toast.**

If using soft-boiled eggs, break them right over the bowl and let the yolk run out over the toast pieces as you scrape the egg from the shell. Then cut up the whites in the bowl and mix into the toast.

Eat with a spoon or fork and knife.

TIPS

We keep a loaf of Ezekiel Low Sodium (dark in color) bread in the freezer. It is a live, sprouting grain, fresh and healthy, hence it must be kept frozen, so unlike normal room temperature bread, it doesn't go stale after a day or so. When we need toast, we cut a slice or two off the frozen loaf and prepare it just as we would any room temperature bread, in a skillet with butter/and or olive oil. In this way we always have good, healthy bread available for any meal. However, other breads can be irresistible in Egg-In-The-Bowl such as an Italian artisan loaf.

Scrambled Eggs

SERVES 2 TO 3 EGGS PER PERSON

You can tell great cooks by the way they handle eggs, particularly scrambled eggs. As simple as some might think they are, by their very nature, scrambled eggs require great skill and care. Think about it; how many restaurants serve great scrambled eggs? They tend to be rubber-like in texture or over-cooked and dry.

Preparing scrambled eggs of the proper consistency is a lost technique for many cooks.

Scrambled eggs are perhaps the one dish we associate with home cooking, next to chicken soup, of course. It is one of the first foods we are given as young children and it is one of the first things we are allowed to eat as we recover from all manner of ills, they are so mild and easy to digest.

Scrambled eggs require ironclad basics. In fact, we learned two important cooking techniques from our scrambled egg preparation, techniques which apply to other foods and recipes.

First, we learned the importance of precise and immediate temperature control in cooking. In this case, we move the skillet on and off the heat to tightly control cooking temperature because if the heat is too high and the eggs cook too quickly, they will get hard and dry. Eggs should be cooked at a steady medium-low temperature to give them a glistening, soft appearance and consistency.

Finally, this is where we learned the importance of the right tools in cooking. In this case the use of a heatproof silicone spatula or wooden paddle (to cleanly lift, fold and stir the egg off the bottom and around the crevices of the pan) and the usefulness of a nonstick skillet, allowing the eggs to cook slowly without clinging to the pan, or worse, hardening or burning.

2 eggs per person (preferably farm-fresh)

Salt and pepper

2 tablespoons butter (olive oil is optional but not quite as tasty)

Optional: 1 teaspoon of very finely chopped herbs (such as chervil or parsley or tarragon or chives, or a combination of these

TOOLS

- Nonstick skillet (a 10-inch for about four eggs and a 12-inch for five or more eggs)
- Heatproof silicone spatula or wooden paddle (available at this writing on Michael Ruhlman's site) to stir and fold the eggs
- Whisk or fork (we prefer the whisk for mixing up the raw eggs which tends to add air to the mixture)
- Optional: diffuser to evenly spread heat over bottom of the pan

1 **Break the eggs into a bowl. Add salt and pepper to taste and beat the eggs with a whisk (or fork) just until a consistent yellow color.** Do not overbeat.

Optional: If you want to be exacting, add the pepper now and add the salt later when the eggs are nearly cooked as some say the early addition of salt can draw moisture out of the eggs.

Optional: if using finely chopped herbs, add them now to the egg mixture.

2 **Meanwhile, melt the butter in a nonstick pan on low or medium low heat.** If you have a diffuser, place it under the pan.

3 **Gently pour the eggs into the pan.** If the eggs form up at once, move the pan off the heat immediately and keep stirring and lifting. It means your flame is too high (see Tip 1).

4 As the eggs heat up and start to form, **stir or lift the eggs continually and gently so none of them stay in contact with the pan too long.** If you moved the pan off the heat because the eggs were forming up too quickly, move it back on after the eggs have clearly stopped cooking so quickly and turn the flame down.

Scrambled Eggs *continued*

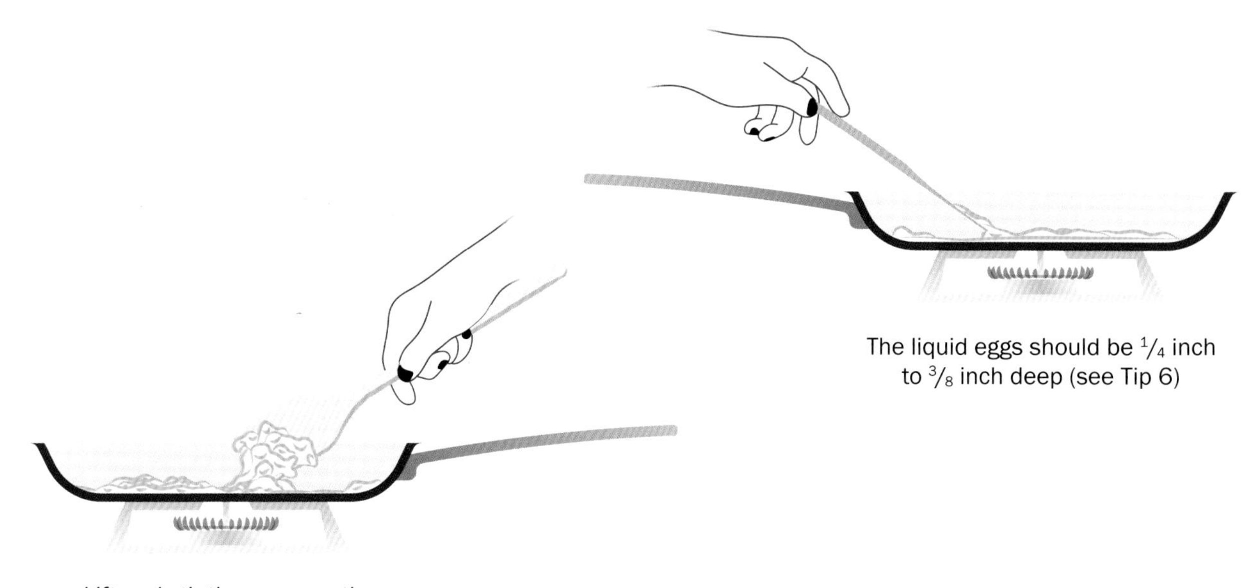

The liquid eggs should be $^{1}/_{4}$ inch to $^{3}/_{8}$ inch deep (see Tip 6)

Lift and stir the eggs gently and continuously

5 Continue to cook the eggs, consistently moving your spatula in broad, long, scooping movements for larger curds or in shorter, faster motions for smaller curds. Make sure to get all of the egg off the bottom and sides of the pan as you stir them or they will harden.

6 When the eggs are firmed up but still glistening, take them off the flame and out of the skillet as they will continue to cook a bit when plated. Do not overcook (see Tip 2).

Optional: Some add a pat of butter near the end. (In the French version referred to below, they stir in cream before cooking. In our version, we don't add any liquid to our eggs to great result.)

TIPS

1. The pan is too hot if the eggs immediately form up or begin cooking upon contact with the pan. The eggs should remain liquid upon contact. If the eggs start to harden too fast, remove the pan from the heat and quickly stir or lift the eggs off the surfaces of the pan with the spatula and keep them moving. Then, adjust the flame to a lower setting.
2. Eggs are subject to carry-over cooking (cooking that continues after the food is removed from a heat source) so be sure and take them off the fire a bit early when they might appear undercooked. This will become second nature with experience.
3. If you like large egg curds, then use a large sweeping, folding motion with the silicone spatula or wooden paddle, and if you like smaller curds, then stir the eggs continually with short motions. You can even use a nonmetallic whisk if you want very small curds, creating an almost soup like consistency, as the French are wont to do. (See About Scrambled Eggs at the end of this recipe)

TIPS, CONTINUED

4. We find the use of a silicone spatula or wooden paddle (available from Michael Ruhlman's website as of this writing) is much more efficient than a wooden spoon at scraping the bottom and sides of a pan, not just for scrambled eggs but for many other foods. Learn to use both of these tools as they are far superior in most applications than the beloved wooden spoon.
5. A very fine method similar to the French method described below in the About section is to set up a medium or large sized pot with an inch or so of water. Put a nonstick or other skillet over it so it rests on top of the pot. Be sure no water touches the bottom of the skillet. Keep the water in the big saucepan at a steady simmer (medium to medium-high flame) and once the steam has warmed the skillet enough, melt the butter. Pour the eggs in and stir and/or lift as in the previous steps above. As described above, the more you move the eggs the creamier and softer they will be. Take the skillet off the steam or turn down the flame a bit to slow the cooking process. The eggs may appear not cooked, as they glisten so much, but they are. This optional method produces a very creamy egg. But may be too rich for some.
6. The size of the skillet matters. If one uses too large a pan, the eggs will spread out too thinly and not cook correctly. You want the liquid eggs to be about ¼" or more in depth. The greater the depth of the liquid eggs, the more your eggs will be creamy and wet. One is "safe" around ¼" to ⅜".

Regardless of which method you choose here, it will take a few times making scrambled eggs to get the hang of it, but once you do, the taste will be magical.

About Scrambled Eggs

Scrambled eggs were not always called "scrambled eggs."

We know from food historians that "scrambled" eggs appeared in different forms from ancient times until the present.

For instance, the ancient Romans mixed their eggs with veggies and then baked them in an oven.

By the 14th century, what we call scrambled eggs were referred to by the Italians in, *Libro della Cucina (The Kitchen Book),* saying that so much is known about the dish, that it is unnecessary to speak about it!

By the 16th century, the English were cooking what they called "Buttered Eggs," a technique consisting of 20 eggs, a pound of butter, some salt, all beaten together, and laid upon toast and baked.

It was in 17th century England that the word "scrambled" was actually used in reference to this type of preparation, and therefore its name. That recipe called for 8 eggs, a pint of cream, beaten and strained through a clean cloth to remove the whey, and then poured into a pan and allowed to "curdle" or scramble as it cooked in a pan.

Leave it to the French to make their version of scrambled eggs an over-the-top elegant dish with a name that almost no one can pronounce. The French came up with *Oeufs Brouillés*, a soft and creamy version of "scrambled eggs," which literally means to "slow down" or to cook very slowly. They are steamed, using a *bain marie* or water bath, employing a saucepan. Constant stirring and a long cooking time creates a soup-like consistency. *Oeufs Brouillés* are traditionally served in a croustade, a toasted hollowed out brioche, or in a deep silver dish surrounded by brioche or croissants.

Three different countries have given us the foundation for the scrambled egg recipe we present to you here.

The Fried Egg

1 TO 2 EGGS PER PERSON

Preparing a fried egg is a melding of art, exacting technique, and taste preference. We prefer our fried eggs cooked slowly with the white firm, rich in flavor, but the yolk runny. Some prefer the slightly crisp, bubbling egg found at American roadside diners and cafés. Once you master the technique below, you can create any variation you wish by changing pans or raising heat levels. Iron skillets are great for higher temp eggs formed with a crispy edge, but start with this recipe and a nonstick pan and you will have the basics to create the fried egg you desire.

Fried eggs are one of those foods that can serve as a main meal, a light snack, a sandwich, or it can be used as an accessory to other dishes, such as over our Peewee Pizza (see recipe, page 16). It is so versatile, that it seems to enhance the flavor of whatever is paired with it.

Many think of the fried egg as one of the great comfort foods and we do too, but mostly it is nourishment with character, character that you, the cook, will give it, depending on your purpose, technique and the additions you choose to accompany it.

The fried egg is always a welcome sight at any table.

1 egg, or more, per person

Salt and pepper

1 to 2 tablespoons butter (or olive oil is optional but not quite as tasty)

TOOLS

- Nonstick skillet, an 8-inch for one or two eggs and a 10-inch for three to four eggs (see Tips 1 and 4)
- Optional: A well-seasoned cast iron or mineral steel skillet. The cast iron should preferably have a smooth surface like the old cast iron (see Old Versus New Cast Iron, page 116). The iron skillet is particularly useful if you want to cook your egg at higher heat and form a crisp edge on the white, but it also works beautifully at a low temperature
- Spatula
- Spoon (to baste the whites with hot butter)
- Optional: copper diffuser (to even the heat under the skillet)

1 **Break each egg into its own bowl.** Discard any egg where the yellow breaks or save it for a sauce or other egg recipes.

2 **Add salt and pepper to taste.**

3 **Meanwhile, heat the butter slowly in a nonstick skillet on medium low or even low heat.** You can always turn the heat up (see Tip 2).

4 **Lowering each bowl near the skillet surface, gently pour the egg(s) into the pan.** The egg(s) should not immediately bubble or even turn white or you have the temperature too high. Pull the skillet off the heat at once if this occurs (see Tip 3).

5 **As the egg slowly cooks, baste the white with the hot butter from the pan.** You can tilt the pan to gather the butter at one side making it easier to scoop up with a small spoon. This will speed the cooking of the whites so the yellow remains soft and does not harden as much as the white of the egg.

Optionally, as the eggs slowly cook, put a lid on the skillet. This will steam the top of the eggs. However, note this method will steam both the yolk and the whites. Basting with butter hurries the cooking of the whites only.

6 **When the white is firm to your liking, remove from the skillet with a spatula or just tip the pan and slide the eggs out.**

Serve over Pan-Fried Toast (see recipe, page 56) atop a fresh salad of greens, over steamed asparagus with our Chicago Cream Sauce (see recipe, page 68), or a shaving of Parmesan cheese, or just all by itself.

TIPS

1. Learn to cook a fried egg in a nonstick pan, first. We have found nonstick skillets are best for eggs as they do not stick to the surface and easily slide in and out. The nonstick pan is perfect for the low heat we use on eggs. Later you can switch to a cast iron skillet if you wish, especially those manufactured with a smooth surface. Some chefs swear by the taste of fried eggs made in an iron skillet. We also use mineral steel pans on a low flame for fried eggs to a great result.
2. In cooking fried eggs we prefer to use a copper diffuser under the skillet that evens the heat out and makes for a more controlled temperature. The secret to a great fried egg is cooking it slowly and evenly.
3. The pan is too hot if the egg immediately firms up or starts becoming white upon contact with the pan. The egg should remain liquid upon contact. If the egg starts to form too quickly, remove the pan from the heat and wait until it cools down. Then, adjust the flame to a lower setting. If you moved the pan off the heat, move it back on after the eggs have clearly stopped cooking so quickly.
4. One of the key factors in cooking fried eggs is the size of the pan. If the pan is too big, the egg whites will spread out and be too thin. While they will cook faster leaving the yellow runny, they will also lose some of their rich flavor. A thicker white gives a more robust flavor than a thin white. Too small a pan and the whites will be too thick and not cook quickly enough to leave the yellow somewhat runny. For 4 eggs, we use a 10-inch skillet, but experiment and find what pan size suits your taste best.

Hard-Boiled Eggs: A Breakthrough

SERVES 1 TO 2 EGGS PER PERSON

We used to think hard-boiled eggs were somewhat boring. In fact, despite our love for eggs, we never really liked hard-boiled eggs all that well; but then an accidental breakthrough a few years ago changed all that and our readers will benefit from this discovery.

We heard, and confirmed, that eggs boiled in water long enough to thorougly cook the yolks resulted in whites that were tough and rubbery. Hence, many people bring them to a boil, quickly take them off the heat and cover them for around 10 to 12 minutes. We tried that with some minor success, but despite this method, they didn't peel easily (even with the ice bath) and more to the point, their taste was only slightly improved.

Then, through an accident, we steamed the eggs as one does vegetables, using a steamer insert. The eggs never touched any boiling water, only steam. After 13 to 15 minutes of steaming, the eggs tasted better, peeled easier and looked brighter than with any other method. There was none of the dreaded gray/green yolk covering either. And if we used farm fresh eggs, especially those from chickens fed a proper diet, the color and taste was magical.

As a general note, fresh eggs, less than a week old, do not peel as easily as eggs a week old or more. After a week or so, air forms between the egg and shell, making it easier to peel. This creates a bit of a dilemma, as fresh eggs are much better tasting in this recipe than older eggs. We believe our steaming technique minimizes some of the difficulty in peeling fresher eggs.

1 or 2 eggs per person

Salt and pepper

TOOLS

- Double boiler with a steamer insert
- Spider or slotted spoon
- A large bowl

TIPS

1. Cool the eggs for several minutes in the cold water (or less if you want to make an egg salad right away (see Tip 2). Dry with paper towels and store the hard-boiled eggs in the refrigerator until ready for use, or eat them at once or make egg salad (see recipe, page 83).
2. We make our egg salad immediately rather than refrigerating the hard-boiled eggs as the residual warmth of the cooked egg absorbs the additional ingredients better and adds a really wonderful taste to the egg salad

1 **Fill the bottom of the pot with about 1 inch of water, put in the insert, and place the lid on top.**

Make sure the waterline is clearly below the steamer basket insert so no water boils up into the basket. No water should touch the eggs.

2 **Turn the heat to medium-high and heat the water to a medium boil.**

3 **Place eggs gently in the steamer in a single layer.** Use a spider or slotted spoon taking care not to let the steam burn your hand.

4 **Steam the eggs for 13 to 15 minutes with the lid in place.** (Timing is dependent on how you like your yolks, softer or harder and cooking altitude, stove and pot.) Leave the top on, the flame on medium-high or medium if the water is too vigorously boiling and wait until 13 to 15 minutes has passed.

5 **Remove eggs with a spider or a slotted spoon and place in a large bowl of cold running water to cool them down a bit.** This will take about 30 seconds or less if you want to eat them warm or hot or use for Egg Salad (see recipe, page 83).

6 **Peel the eggs.** If egg peeling is difficult, roll the egg on your counter and try to grab the membrane which surrounds the white and pull the shell away from the egg, discarding the shell bits.

7 **Run each peeled egg under cold water again, rinsing off any shell fragments that may have adhered.**

Eat immediately, make egg salad or another hard-boiled egg recipe, or don't peel and dry off the shells and store in the refrigerator.

Soft-Boiled Eggs

SERVES 1 TO 2 EGGS PER PERSON

Soft-boiled eggs conjure up visions of light fare when we are watching our waistline, but to the contrary and fortunately so, they are also a wonderful comfort food.

Whether serving the soft-boiled egg for breakfast, lunch or dinner, it offers an opportunity to vary the accompaniments depending on how full a meal you want to eat. We love it at its most glorious as the star of Egg-In-The-Bowl (see recipe, page 74). However, and whenever you decide to eat this most perfect food, the exact art of preparing it is the secret to a magically delicious soft-boiled egg.

Because of our breakthrough in steaming hard-boiled eggs (see Hard-Boiled Eggs: A Breakthrough, page 80) we naturally applied it to the soft-boiled egg to great result.

Steam the eggs as you do vegetables, using a steamer insert. The eggs never touch any boiling water, only steam.

This is one of life's great pleasures, whether you are in good health or in need of an easily digestible food, soft-boiled eggs allow us to reminisce over wonderful memories of a perfectly cooked yolk swaddled in a soft, creamy white coat, the perfect medium for dipping toast or bacon.

1 or 2 eggs per person

Salt and pepper

TOOLS

- Pot or saucepan with a steamer insert and top
- Spider or slotted spoon
- Sharp knife or egg scissors
- Small egg spoon

1 **Fill the bottom of the pot with about 1 inch of water and place the insert in and the lid on top.** Make sure the waterline is clearly below the steamer basket insert so no waters boils up into the basket. No water should be touching the egg(s).

2 **Turn the heat to medium-high and heat the water to a medium boil.**

3 **Place eggs gently in the steamer in a single layer.** Use a spider or slotted spoon taking care not to let the steam burn your hand.

4 **Steam the eggs for 5 ½ to 6 ½ minutes with the lid in place.** Timing will vary with altitude, stove, pot, or taste.

5 **Remove eggs with a spider or a slotted spoon and place in a large bowl of cold running water to cool them down a bit, about 30 seconds or so.** You want them cool enough to handle, but still warm.

6 **Cut off the top of the egg** (see Tip 2) **and serve as suggested below.** If serving out of the shell, merely cut into the egg halfway down the shell and break open, allowing the egg to flow out. Remove any remainder with a spoon.

7 **Season with salt and pepper as desired.**

Serve with or on Pan-Fried Toast (see recipe, page 56), with bacon (see recipe, page 61), fried potatoes (see recipe, page 48), sliced tomatoes, over greens or as desired. A slight sprinkling of orange vinegar adds a nice sharp contrast.

Soft-Boiled Eggs *continued*

TIPS

1. The cooking time for soft-boiled eggs will vary depending on altitude, stove, pot, and your preference for loose or firm eggs. You want a medium boil on the water under the insert, so adjust your flame accordingly. If you keep the above constant you will find the exact length of time to cook the eggs through trial and error, which should fall between 5 ½ to 6 ½ minutes, depending on your taste and other factors.
2. If you do not have a commercial soft-boiled egg cutter, the following technique will take some practice, but works well: merely tap the side of the egg with a sharp knife (creating a crack), or pierce the egg shell with a sharp knife close to the top. Then slice into the eggshell by carefully moving the knife along the crack. Lift up on the top of the egg revealing the soft yolk. If using the eggshell as a container use a small spoon or strips of toast to remove and eat the egg. If serving outside of the shell, merely cut into the egg halfway down the shell and break open, allowing the egg to flow out. Remove any remainder with a spoon.

Egg Salad

SERVES 4–6

Eggs and mayonnaise go together as naturally as milk and cookies or peanut butter and jelly.

A really great egg salad is nearly impossible to find. Many of the egg salads we have eaten tended to have too much mayonnaise, often with too finely chopped eggs. This overwhelms the otherwise rich flavor of the egg and produces a mushy texture.

With extensive work we finally created a recipe we feel is just right...due to three discoveries:

First, we found if we steamed the eggs, never letting them touch water, they tasted better and peeled more easily.

Secondly we found if we used small amounts of well-chosen ingredients (including the mayonnaise) then the egg flavor was retained and even enhanced, resulting in a salad with nuance and interest.

Third, we found the egg salad tasted better if, after making it, we let the flavors marry up for several hours or overnight.

Egg salad as the crowning glory of a green salad with avocado, cucumber, and tomato slices, in a sandwich, on top of crackers, on Pan-Fried Toast (see recipe, page 56), or as a snack all by itself, is healthy and delicious.

12 eggs (farm fresh and if possible less than 10 days old)

1 stalk of celery, about 6 to 7 inches long, chopped, but not too finely

1 thin slice of red onion, chopped finely, about ¾ tablespoon

2 heaping tablespoons of mayonnaise (we prefer Hellman's) or just enough to dampen the chopped egg and make the mixture fluffy (However, it is noted this is a matter of taste for each cook)

¼ to ½ teaspoon of Dijon style mustard (or none if preferred)

Dash of cayenne

Salt and pepper

TOOLS

- A 4 to 5-quart stainless steel saucepan and cover
- Steaming insert
- Spider
- Large bowl
- 2 table knives
- Spatula or wooden spoon for mixing
- Glass jar(s) for storage and to marry up the flavors

1 **Fill the bottom of the pot with about 1 inch of water and place the insert in and the lid on top.** Make sure the water line is clearly below the steamer basket insert so no waters boils up into the basket. No water should be touching the bottom of the insert. Place the lid on top with the insert in place.

2 **Turn the heat to medium high and heat the water to a medium boil.**

3 **Place eggs gently in the steamer in a single layer.** Use a spider or slotted spoon taking care not to let the steam burn your hand.

4 **Steam the eggs for 13 to 15 minutes with the lid in place.** (Timing is dependent on how you like your yolks, softer or harder.) Leave the top on, the flame on medium-high or medium if the water is too vigorously boiling and wait until 13 to 15 minutes has passed (see illustration 1).

5 **While the eggs are cooking, prepare all the other ingredients per the ingredients list.** Most efficiently, put each in a bowl ready to use.

6 **Remove eggs with a spider or a slotted spoon and place in a large bowl of cold running water to cool them down a bit.** Do so for about 30 seconds or more (see illustration 2).

7 **Peel the eggs.** If egg peeling is difficult, roll the egg on your counter and try to grab the membrane which surrounds the white and pull the shell away from the egg, discarding the shell bits.

8 **Run each peeled egg under cold water again, rinsing off any shell fragments that may have adhered.**

9 **In a large dry bowl, gently chop the warm eggs with two knives until the yolks and whites are somewhat broken up, but not finely.** The whites and yellow should be about the size of a nickel or even larger. We found if one chops the eggs more than this their flavor is greatly reduced (see illustration 3).

Egg Salad *continued*

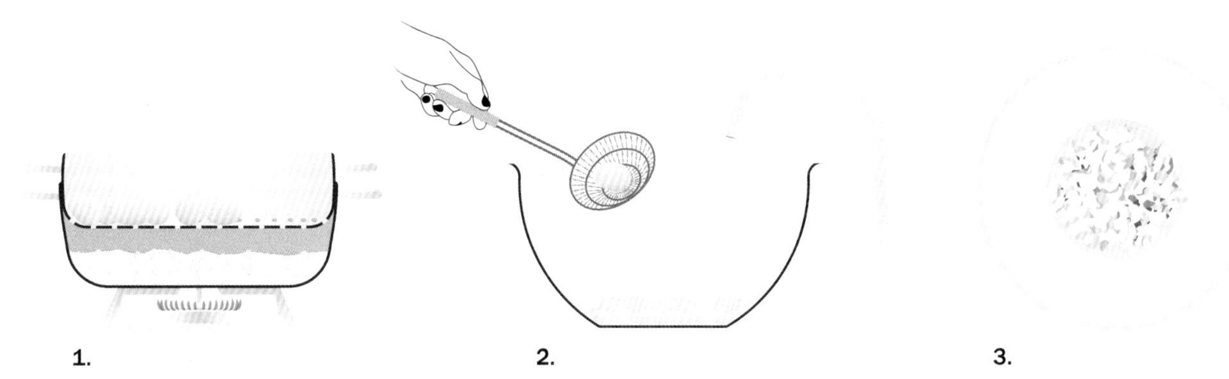

10 Add the mayo, chopped onion, chopped celery, salt, pepper, cayenne and mustard (optional) and fold in gently being careful not to further break up the eggs.

We prefer a drier egg salad, but if you wish a wetter one, by all means add more mayo. However, we caution you to do a little at a time as it doesn't take much too over-do it which will produce a mushy egg salad. And you will lose the taste of the eggs, overwhelmed with mayonnaise.

11 Taste and further correct the seasoning, noting that this recipe needs time to marry up.

12 Place in a glass jar or container with a tight lid and refrigerate for many hours or preferably overnight. If possible re-taste after that and further season as needed and/or add a little more mayo to freshen.

Serve on top of salad greens, on Pan-Fried Toast (see recipe, page 56), or with crackers.

TIPS

1. The cooking time for hard-boiled eggs will vary depending on altitude, stove, pot, and your preference. You want a medium boil on the water under the insert so adjust your flame accordingly. If you keep the above constant you will find the exact length of time to cook the eggs through trial and error, which should fall between 13 and 15 minutes.
2. Cool the eggs only as long as needed to make them easily handleable so they can be peeled and chopped while still warm.
3. We make our egg salad immediately rather than refrigerating the hard-boiled eggs as the residual warmth of the cooked egg absorbs the additional ingredients better and adds a really wonderful taste to the egg salad. After all ingredients are added and combined, we do let the flavors marry up for several hours or preferably overnight before eating.

About Egg Salad

The French invented mayonnaise around 1756. Shortly thereafter, evidence of eggs mixed with mayonnaise, vegetables, such as celery, onion, and other herbs and spices, appeared as luncheon fare. Wherever lettuce and tomatoes appeared on a cold plate, eggs seemed to appear, too; whole and blanketed with mayonnaise, sliced, or chopped and mixed with onion and celery, salt and pepper. The famous American trio of luncheon salads we find in early cookbooks and on tearoom menus consisted of egg salad, chicken salad, and tuna fish salad. Egg salad remains an American favorite for breakfast on toast, as picnic fare, or on salad greens.

A SWEET ENDING

All you need is love, but a little chocolate now and then doesn't hurt.

— CHARLES M. SCHULTZ

Oatmeal Raisin Cookies

MAKES ABOUT TWO-DOZEN LARGE COOKIES

These cookies have been a part of Carol's baking repertoire for many years. They are so flavorful and fragrant that her son has come to expect the aroma of the freshly baked cookies to fill the air and greet him when he comes to Chicago to visit! He is never disappointed.

The recipe is a joy because all of the mixing is done in one saucepan. When the mixing is complete, and it is time for the actual baking, we suggest using a silicone baking mat on each sheet pan to avoid buttering the pan's surface and therefore frying the cookies. Baking mats also make the removal of the cookies easier when they have cooled. You will need about 10 minutes for cooling these cookies. If you remove the cookies too soon, they will break apart.

1 stick of unsalted butter

1 ½ cups light brown sugar, tightly packed into a measuring cup. (Do not use organic brown sugar as the result will be a very different textured cookie)

1 egg

3 tablespoons flour

½ teaspoon baking powder

¼ teaspoon salt

½ teaspoon vanilla extract, the best brand you can buy

1 ½ cups oatmeal such as Quaker Old Fashioned Oats (not Quick Oats)

½ to 1 cup raisins or to taste

TOOLS

- A 3 to 4 quart saucepan
- 1 large whisk
- A wooden paddle or spoon
- 2 half-sheet pans with a silicone baking mat to fit each pan
- Spatula
- Cooling rack
- Optional: diffuser to gently melt butter

1 **Preheat oven to 350 degrees.**

2 **In a large saucepan, melt butter over medium-low heat** (or if using a diffuser, over medium heat).

3 **When the butter is completely melted, add the brown sugar, stirring until well mixed.**

4 **Add the egg to the mixture and immediately beat with a whisk until smooth.**
Do not allow the egg to sit on top of the sugar and butter mixture, as it will begin to cook, thus compromising its smooth addition.

5 **Remove from heat and add the flour, baking powder, salt, and the vanilla. Blend well with a wooden spoon.**

6 **Stir in oats and raisins and combine well.**

7 **Drop 1 heaping tablespoon of dough per cookie onto the sheet pans.**
Do not press the dough down. Note: you must allow six cookies only to each sheet pan. Therefore, make two rows per pan, three cookies per row. The dough will spread as it cooks and unless you arrange the dough as shown in the illustration, it will run together in one big gooey mess.

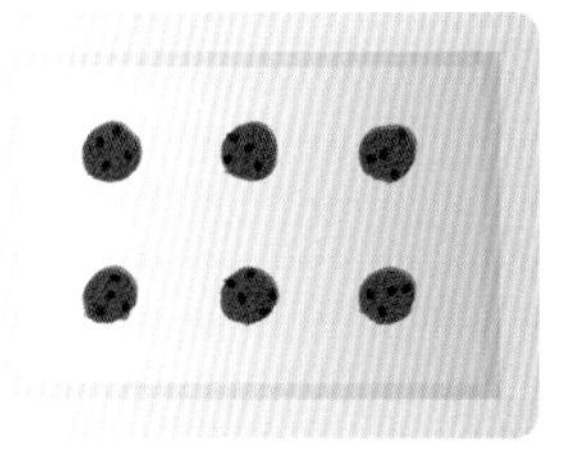

8 **Bake at 350 degrees until browned and the dough at the center of the cookie is set, about 8 to 10 minutes.**
Check the baking process after 8 minutes or so to be sure the cookies do not over-brown. This variation in time allows for variation in oven temperature.

9 **Remove the cookies from the oven and allow them to rest on the sheet pans for about 10 to 15 minutes.** Remember that removing them too soon will cause them to break apart.

10 **Using a spatula, remove to a cooling rack or parchment paper to cool.**

Mocha Brownies

MAKES ABOUT 24 BROWNIES

Love dark chocolate? Love coffee? This is an unusual brownie with a character all of its own. It is flavored with coffee, dark chocolate, and loads of vanilla to create a moist, luscious mocha treat. Not too sweet, not too rich (even with all of that butter and brown sugar!), people just go crazy over these.

Rather than using commercial chocolate chips for this brownie, we much prefer Scharffen Berger's bittersweet chocolate, hand cut into chunks, creating a richer texture and flavor.

The joyful part of the recipe? It is all mixed in one saucepan.

To make this an over-the-top rich and more decadent dessert, serve it with a scoop of vanilla ice cream or a spoonful of whipped cream. This brownie always makes a hit as a dessert all by itself or on a platter with other cookies and chocolate truffles.

2 tablespoons instant coffee powder (not crystals)

1 tablespoon hot water

1 ½ sticks of unsalted butter

2 cups of dark brown sugar

2 eggs

2 tablespoons high quality vanilla extract

2 cups unbleached all purpose flour

2 teaspoons baking powder

½ teaspoon salt

1 cup Scharffen Berger's bittersweet chocolate, about 4 ½ oz, and cut into medium-sized chunks, about the size of a dime

TOOLS

- 3 to 4-quart sauce pan
- Whisk
- Hand-held mixer
- Wooden spoon or paddle
- Off-set or rubber spatula
- 9-inch by 13-inch baking pan
- Cooling rack
- Knife or bench scraper to cut cooked brownies
- Optional: diffuser to melt butter

1 **Dissolve the coffee powder in the hot water.**

2 **Butter the sides and bottom of the baking pan and set aside.**

3 **Melt butter in the saucepan over medium heat** on a diffuser (if you have one). **Add the brown sugar and whisk in.**

4 **Add the dissolved coffee to the butter and brown sugar and whisk until smooth.**

5 **Allow to cool to room temperature in the same pan.**

6 **Preheat the oven to 350 degrees.**

7 **While the butter/sugar/coffee mixture is cooling, take about 4 ½ ounces of Scharffen Berger's bittersweet chocolate and using a sharp chef's knife or meat pounder, break the chocolate into medium-sized chunks about the size of a dime or to your liking.**

8 **When the butter/sugar/coffee mixture is cool, beat in the eggs and vanilla with a hand-held mixer right in the same saucepan.**

9 **Sift flour, baking powder, and salt together and add to the batter with a wooden spoon or paddle and combine well.**

10 **Stir in the chocolate chunks and combine well with a wooden spoon.**

11 **Pour the mixture into the buttered 9-inch by 13-inch baking pan and spread the batter evenly with an off-set or rubber spatula.**

12 **Bake at 350 degrees for 20 to 25 minutes.** Do NOT overbake. As the brownies cool, they will continue to cook, known as carryover cooking. If your oven is a true 350 degrees, then 25 minutes is enough. Insert a toothpick or knife point and if it comes out clean, then you know it is done.

13 **Cool completely, cut into squares.**

Chocolate Mousse

SERVES 6

There is no more elegant finish to an extraordinary dinner than a dark chocolate dessert. This mousse recipe is the result of extensive testing and refinement and the taste is exceptional. It is rich and decadent and no matter how full our guests, they always have room for a small ramekin of this mousse. We serve it with whipped cream on top and optionally, a sprig of mint with a few red raspberries on the side.

A popular dessert of the '70's, it has made a return as a vintage treat and one that is deservedly just as popular as it was 40 years ago.

9-ounce bar of unsweetened chocolate, we prefer Scharffen Berger Chocolate (see Tip 1)

6 ounces of Scharffen Berger semisweet chocolate

(Both bars cut into small pieces or better yet, shaved it into thin ribbons or pieces using a very sharp chef's knife)

2 tablespoons unsalted butter

1 cup sugar (we use superfine or castor sugar in many of our dessert recipes to create extra smoothness)

6 egg yolks, lightly beaten

6 tablespoons liqueur, such as Grand Marnier, Cointreau, or Scotch whiskey or to taste

6 egg whites, at room temperature

Ingredients for the Optional Garnish

Heavy whipping cream

Mint leaves or sprigs

Red raspberries or other seasonal fruit of your choice

TOOLS

- 1 sauce pan (3 to 4 quart)
- 2 large glass bowls
- A hand or standing mixer
- Medium-sized whisk
- Large wooden spoon
- 6 to 8 half-cup ramekins or other attractive containers such as a martini glass, or one medium sized serving bowl

1 **Bring an inch or more of water just to a simmer in a 3 to 4 quart sauce pan,** large enough to hold a heatproof bowl.

2 **Do your *mise en place* for all ingredients** (see Tip 2).

3 **With a sharp knife, shave the chocolate or cut it into small chunks.** We find that shaving it allows the chocolate to melt faster and contributes to a smooth texture (see Tip 3).

4 **In a large bowl** (we use a thick heatproof glass bowl) **mix the chocolate, butter, and ½ cup sugar together so they are evenly distributed.**

5 **Place the heatproof bowl on the saucepan of barely simmering water.** The water must not touch the bottom of the bowl (see Tip 6).

6 **Let the chocolate heat without stirring until it completely melts.** If you stir it, the chocolate may seize and become unworkable. The chocolate may take up to an hour to melt.

7 **Remove the bowl from the heat and move it to a counter top or work space and gently stir in lightly beaten egg yolks. Then stir in the liqueur.** Set aside.

8 **In the other large bowl, beat the egg whites with the mixer until stiff peaks form.** Use an impeccably clean and spotless bowl. Again we use a thick glass one with no trace of grease or oil (see Tip 4 and 5).

9 **Gradually beat in remaining ½ cup of sugar and continue beating until glossy and stiff peaks form again.**

10 **Hand whisk about one-third of the egg whites into the other bowl with the chocolate, whisking vigorously in order to lighten the mixture.**

11 **Gently fold the remaining whites into the chocolate mixture with a wooden paddle, spoon, or rubber spatula.**

12 **Pour the mousse into a serving bowl, ramekins, or other pretty serving containers and cover tightly with plastic wrap.**

Refrigerate overnight to allow the flavors to develop, preferably for 24 hours. We have even allowed the flavors to develop as long as three days and it just becomes richer and more flavorful with time.

Optional garnish: serve with whipped cream on top garnished with a mint sprig and a few red raspberries or fruit of your choice on the side. Peaches, black raspberries, and blueberries are all good choices and very compatible with chocolate.

TIPS

1. We prefer and recommend Scharffen Berger chocolate for all of our chocolate desserts.
2. We suggest that you do a *mise en place* for all ingredients except the garnish. *Mise en place* is a French term used by chefs to refer to the preparation of all ingredients before beginning any recipe. Each ingredient is placed in its own prep bowl and assembled on a cutting board or suitable surface. As you follow the recipe directions, each ingredient has been measured and gathered in one place, making your cooking more accurate and more efficient. If you get in the habit of doing the *mise en place* each time you cook, you will see its advantage.
3. To melt fairly large amounts of chocolate, as in this recipe, it will melt faster and more evenly if you chop it into small pieces first or, better yet, shave it into thin pieces using a sharp knife.
4. When separating eggs, and especially if you are directed to beat the whites into peaks, be certain that not one dot of yolk is in the bowl containing the whites or the whites will not whip.
5. Whenever beating egg whites, be sure that the whites are at room temperature and the bowl you use is absolutely free of oily residue or grease, otherwise the whites will not become stiff.
6. When melting chocolate, use a very low flame and never stir or disturb the chocolate in any way, it will seize or stiffen and become unworkable. It cannot be resurrected. Leave it alone.

Crêpe Pastry

SERVES 6

This elegant and eye-popping dish is a family favorite for weekend brunch or as a dessert anytime. Carol adapted it after a French family's recipe for their children, minus the alcohol, of course.

When brought to the table, people gasp at its distinctive presentation, the height that is achieved with some twelve to fifteen crêpes, stacked and oozing butter, brown sugar, and cinnamon. When you cut the pastry into wedges, all of those layers reveal themselves. The fragrance of the ingredients along with the brûléed cloak (sugar broiled to a crisp, caramel brown) is mouthwatering—pure ambrosia.

This dish promises to acquire celebrity status at any meal.

Ingredients for the Batter

¾ cup of whole milk

¾ cup of water

3 large eggs

1 tablespoon granulated sugar

3 tablespoons Grand Marnier (orange liqueur)

1 cup flour

5 tablespoons melted unsalted butter

Ingredients for the Completed Crêpes

1 stick of unsalted butter

½ cup of light brown sugar (more if needed, depending on how many crêpes you end up with)

Cinnamon to taste

1 tablespoon of white granulated sugar (for crunch)

TOOLS

- Blender (a Vitamix or comparable)
- Measuring cup
- Small nonstick pan or a small crêpe pan
- A long, narrow spatula for turning the crêpes
- A Pyrex pie plate (about 12-inch) or other ovenproof round serving dish

1 **Place all of the ingredients of the batter in the jar of the blender in the order in which they are listed** (in the batter ingredients section) **and blend until smooth and well-mixed, about 2 minutes.** If bits of flour stick to the jar, turn off the machine and scrape the sides with a rubber spatula.

2 **Pour into a Mason jar or other glass container, refrigerate for several hours or overnight.** Before cooking, give the jar a good shake to remix the ingredients.

3 **Do your *mise en place*** (see Tip 2). Have the pie plate, spatula, butter, brown sugar, and cinnamon at your side on a cutting board or other flat surface placed near you at the stove, to your right or left, whichever is more convenient for you.

4 **Heat the crêpe pan or nonstick skillet, melt a bit of butter in the bottom and when hot, but not smoking, pour about ¼ cup of the batter into the center of the pan, swirling the pan with your wrist in a circular motion to evenly distribute the batter, thinly covering the entire bottom surface of the pan** (see Tip 1).

5 **Allow the crêpe to cook until the edges brown and begin to curl.** The crêpe is now ready to flip. **Using a long spatula, carefully turn it over.** You can use your fingers to do this, but then you need to have what Sara Moulton refers to as "asbestos fingers!"

6 **Continue to cook the second side until brown, but not crisp.**

7 **Remove to the pie plate and immediately pour another ¼ cup of batter into the skillet repeating steps 4, 5 and 6 above.**

8 **While the next crêpe cooks, take a little butter and smear it on the cooked crêpe you removed to the pie plate. Then sprinkle about 1 teaspoon of brown sugar all over the surface of the crêpe. And finally, sprinkle some cinnamon on top of that.**

9 **Repeat the process, adding a bit of butter to the pan as needed, piling the finished crêpes on top of each other until you have a stack of about 12 to 15 crêpes with cinnamon and brown sugar in between each one.** This can be done in advance and refrigerated at this point or if using that very day, it can sit on your counter until just before you are ready to serve it.

10 **When the last crêpe is in place, sprinkle with cinnamon and white sugar.**

11 **Before serving, bring the pastry to room temperature if it was refrigerated. Then place the "Crêpe Pastry" under the broiler for a very few seconds, and caramelize the sugar on the top crêpe, making sure it does not burn (or use a small kitchen torch.) Serve immediately.**

An optional thought is to serve it as a dessert accompanied by a small scoop of vanilla ice cream.

TIPS

1. Traditionally, the first crêpe, "seasons" the pan and you will want to throw it out after it is cooked. Use this first one to practice the technique of pouring and quickly swirling it to cover the bottom of the pan.
2. *Mise en place* is a French term used by chefs to refer to the preparation of all ingredients before beginning any recipe. Each ingredient is placed in its own prep bowl and assembled on a cutting board or suitable surface. As you follow the recipe directions, each ingredient has been measured and gathered in one place, making your cooking more accurate and more efficient. If you get in the habit of doing the *mise en place* each time you cook, you will see its advantage

Pavlova

SERVES ABOUT 10 PEOPLE

There are some desserts that are perfect for the summer; others clearly come under the heading of winter food. We love seasonal food, but here is one that is a dessert for all seasons, named, so they say, after the famous Russian ballerina, Anna Pavlova when she visited Australia and New Zealand in the early 20th century.

Traditionally, it begins with a meringue shell, a beautiful, sweet confection that is essentially a platform made of whipped egg whites, sugar, and vanilla.

It is then topped by a layer of whipped cream followed by berries and fruit of all kinds, making a gorgeous multi-colored mosaic.

This is a dessert that truly impresses anyone lucky enough to be invited for dinner!

For the meringue shell

8 egg whites (no specs of yolk!) at room temperature

Pinch of salt

2 ½ cups super-fine sugar

4 tablespoons cornstarch

2 teaspoons white wine vinegar

1 teaspoon vanilla extract

Ingredients for the fruit

About 3 ½ pints of berries of your choice. We prefer lots of blueberries, raspberries, blackberries, kiwi fruit, strawberries, and sometimes bananas, or any combination of them.

½ cup sugar

1 tablespoon Balsamic vinegar

1 pint of whipping cream, chilled

2 tablespoons of honey

Optional: Vanilla bean (for whipped cream)

TOOLS

- Standing or handheld mixer
- Large bowl
- Parchment paper
- Sheet pan
- Silicone spatula or offset spatula

Directions for Meringue Shell

1 **Heat oven to 300 degrees.**

2 **Line a sheet pan with parchment paper.**

3 **Beat egg whites and salt on medium high speed until the whites thicken and peaks form, about 3 to 4 minutes.**

4 **Add sugar a little at a time on medium speed and when all of it has been added, turn the mixer from medium to high in order to fully incorporate the sugar.**

5 **Add cornstarch to the egg whites and whisk it by hand to blend.**

6 **Then add vinegar and whisk by hand.**

7 **Finally, add the vanilla extract and whisk in.**

8 **Using a spatula or better yet, an offset spatula, pile the egg white mixture in the center of the parchment paper or baking mat and spread it in a circle or rectangular shape about 7 to 10 inches across and about 2 inches high.** Make the sides slightly higher to get a bit of a bowl effect so you can nest the fruit in it later.

9 **Put the meringue in the oven.**

10 **Bake the meringue for 1½ hours.**

11 **When cooked, turn oven off and prop oven door open. Let meringue cool down completely.**

Meringue can be stored uncovered for several hours.

Preparing The Fruit

As the time approaches to serve the Pavlova:

1 **Rinse berries, place in large bowl, add sugar and vinegar.**

2 **Gently and evenly mix together with your impeccably clean hands.** Do not mash the fruit when mixing.

Set aside to sit (macerate) for 30 minutes.

Preparing The Whipped Cream

1 **Pour whipping cream into large** (preferably cold) **bowl.**

Optional: One can scrape seeds from a vanilla bean into the cream.

2 **Using your stand or hand mixer, whisk cream until soft peaks form, about two or more minutes.**

3 **Add two tablespoons of honey or to taste and briefly continue to mix until honey is incorporated.**

4 **Chill until ready to assemble.**

Assemblage

1 **Place meringue shell on large serving platter.**

2 **Mound the whipped cream in center and spread evenly over shell, creating a slight bowl effect to place the fruit in..**

3 **Fully drain macerated berries or other fruits of their juices.** If you do not, the meringue will collapse or become soggy.

4 **Spoon drained berries over whipped cream,** adding any other fruit at this time, such as a fresh, sliced banana.

Flourless Chocolate Cake

SERVES 6 TO 8

One of the great desserts of all time, the basics for this recipe were passed down by Jonathan's mother, a wonderful Chicago cook (and art collector). Warmth, richness, and class describe both the dessert and the mother.

The secret to this recipe is the use of really fine quality chocolate and the precise control of technique and baking time. Making it a day in advance will ensure that all flavors develop, but fresh out of the oven, it is pretty irresistible, especially still warm with vanilla ice cream on the side, a sprig of fresh mint and even three or four fresh raspberries.

Very elegant!

4 ounces unsweetened chocolate, we highly recommend Scharffen Berger which results in a dense, richly flavored cake (see Tip 1)

8 ounces semi-sweet chocolate (also Scharffen Berger)

1 tablespoon Cognac

½ cup unsalted butter

½ teaspoon vanilla

¼ teaspoon salt

½ cup superfine sugar divided into two ¼ cup portions

4 eggs separated (with absolutely no yolk in the whites and no white in the yolks)

2 tablespoons soft butter to coat springform pan

Superfine sugar for coating springform pan

Optional for garnish: Confectioners Sugar (to sprinkle over finished cake), fresh mint, whipped cream, or vanilla ice cream

TOOLS

- Large heatproof glass bowl
- Pot large enough to hold the heatproof bowl (for melting the chocolate)
- Chef's knife
- Hand or stand mixer
- Wooden spoon or paddle
- Whisk
- Large rubber spatula
- Medium bowl (for the yolks)
- Large bowl (for the egg whites)
- Springform pan

1 **Shave or chop the chocolate into fine pieces so it will melt evenly and easily** (see Tip 3).

2 **Put the finely chopped or shaved chocolate and cognac in top of a double boiler or better yet, in a thick, spotless (preferably glass), large heatproof bowl on top of a pot with slightly simmering water** (see Tip 6).

Do not let the water boil even gently. Allow about an hour for this, letting the chocolate heat and melt gently. Do not stir or touch the melting chocolate or it will seize and become unworkable. Leave it alone to slowly melt by itself.

3 **Preheat oven to 425 degrees** (see Tip 8), **and do your *mise en place* but do not beat any of the eggs yet** (see Tip 2).

4 **In the meantime, cut the butter (1 stick) into four even parts and then each part into small squares.** This is so that when each part is added to the chocolate, it melts more quickly and evenly.

5 **When the chocolate is fully melted, remove from heat and add one part of the cut-up butter, blending it thoroughly before adding the next until all the cut-up butter is blended into the chocolate.**

6 **Using a wooden paddle or spoon, stir in ¼ cup of the superfine sugar combining it with the chocolate/butter mixture until the sugar is dissolved.**

7 **In a separate medium bowl, beat the egg yolks until light and thickened, using a hand electric beater.**

8 **Very gradually whisk the egg yolks into the chocolate mixture (so it does not separate). Add vanilla and gently stir in.**

9 **In another (third) large bowl (completely free of grease and oil residue) beat egg whites and salt until foamy.** Use an electric beater (see Tips 4 and 5).

10 **Gradually add the remaining ¼ cup of superfine sugar to the egg whites, while beating them. Beat until stiff.**

11 **Using a large rubber spatula, gently drop about half of the beaten egg whites onto the chocolate batter. Cut through the egg white mixture down into the chocolate and bring it gently up and over the whites. Continue this gentle, precise action, rotating the bowl as you gently fold the mixture together so no visible white is left** (see Tip 7).

12 **Take the second half of the egg whites and repeat step #11 exactly.**

13 **Smear soft butter over the internal sides and bottom of the spring form pan. Sprinkle superfine sugar around the sides and bottom of the buttered spring form pan. Shake around the sides, tilting pan until the sugar is evenly distributed.**

14 **Pour the chocolate mixture into buttered and sugared 9-inch springform pan.**

15 **Bake in a preheated 425 degree oven for 13 minutes for a moist, fudge-like result, 15 minutes for a drier cake-like result, or 14 minutes for something in between.** Avoid opening the oven during cooking. Your timing may vary due to different ovens, baking pan thickness, and altitude.

16 **Allow to cool if not serving immediately.** The cake will fall slightly, then it will firm as it cools. Sprinkle the top with powdered sugar.

Optional: Serve with freshly whipped cream or vanilla ice cream and a sprig of fresh mint.

May be made a day or two in advance as it keeps well at least that long in its springform pan covered with tin foil and at room temperature.

TIPS

1. We prefer and recommend Scharffen Berger chocolate for all of our chocolate desserts.
2. We suggest that you do a *mise en place* for all ingredients except the garnish. A *mise en place* means to prepare and measure all ingredients and place them in small "prep" bowls before beginning this or any recipe. It is efficient and will prepare you for each addition rather than having to stop to prepare the next step, especially important in recipes that require egg whites.
3. To melt fairly large amounts of chocolate, as in this recipe, it will melt faster and more evenly if you chop it into small pieces first or, better yet, shave it into thin pieces.
4. When separating eggs, and especially if you are directed to beat the whites into peaks, be certain that not one dot of yolk is in the bowl containing the whites or the whites will not whip.
5. Whenever beating egg whites, be sure that the whites are at room temperature and the bowl you use is absolutely free of oily residue or grease, otherwise the whites will not become stiff.
6. When melting chocolate, use a very low flame and never stir or disturb it in any way, it will seize or stiffen and become unworkable. It cannot be resurrected. Leave it alone.
7. The reason you want to gently fold the beaten, fluffy egg whites into the chocolate mixture, and not the other way around, is that the chocolate is very heavy and so folding the whites into it prevents the whites from deflating. You want as much volume as possible in the mixture.
8. It takes about 20 to 25 minutes to pre-heat an oven to the desired temperature. We suggest, therefore, turning on the oven early, see step 2 of this recipe.

Schnecken (or Sticky Buns)

MAKES 48

These yeasty, sweet breakfast rolls, served warm, are made from a recipe, long held in Carol's family. German in origin and resembling the spiral shape of a snail, "schnecken" (the German word for snail) are of the yeast dough family of breads, which means that as they bake, their aroma will truly define comfort food for you, especially on a cold day.

Redolent of brown sugar, cinnamon, butter and pecans, served warmed, they are irresistible. We have had repeated requests from friends to include this recipe in our cookbook, they are that wonderfully delicious.

If you are a baker, you will find this recipe reminiscent of your grandmother. If you are new to baking, jump in and try it. It is worth it when they are done. Promise.

Ingredients for the Dough

½ cup lukewarm milk

2 envelopes dry yeast

5 cups all-purpose flour

2 sticks unsalted butter

½ cup sugar

A pinch of salt

1 cup sour cream

3 eggs, lightly beaten

½ stick of room temperature butter (to grease bottom and sides of each muffin cup, 48 muffin cups total)

Ingredients for Each Muffin Cup

1 teaspoon melted butter (2 sticks total for 48 muffin tins)

1 teaspoon brown sugar (1 cup for 48 muffin tins)

1 teaspoon white corn syrup (1 cup for 48 muffin tins)

1 teaspoon pecan chips (1 cup for 48 muffin tins)

Ingredients for the Paste

2 sticks of butter, softened to spreadable consistency

2 tablespoons cinnamon

1 cup brown sugar

TOOLS

- Stand mixer
- Small saucepan
- Rubber spatula
- Large mixing bowl
- Medium-sized mixing bowl
- Plastic wrap
- 4 muffin tins with 12 cups each
- An offset spatula
- 4 Clean dish towels
- Tin foil

General Directions

The night before baking the Schnecken, mix the dough ingredients and refrigerate overnight. The second day you will prepare the pans, make the sticky topping, cut the dough into Schnecken, allow the rolls to rise, and bake them until they are golden brown.

The Night Before Baking—Making the Dough

1 **In a small saucepan, heat the milk taking care that the milk is just lukewarm.** If the milk is too hot, it will kill the yeast when added. If it is too cool, the yeast will not dissolve and begin its reaction. Remove from heat.

2 **Sprinkle the yeast over the lukewarm milk and allow it to sit for a bit.**

3 **Then take a fork and stir the powdered yeast into the milk.** The mixture will appear gray and gummy. Do not over mix. Allow the mixture to rest while you begin the dough preparation.

4 **In a stand mixer fitted with the paddle attachment begin mixing the flour and butter.** Start on low so the flour does not spray all over, and then increase the speed to medium so it crumbles the flour and butter to resemble peas.

5 Switch out the paddle attachment to the dough hook attachment. **Add the sugar, salt, sour cream, and eggs to the butter and flour-crumbled mixture. Mix again to combine.** The mixture should now look more like dough.

6 **Add the yeast mixture and mix thoroughly using the stand mixer.**

7 **Place in a glass bowl, cover the bowl with plastic wrap and refrigerate overnight.**

The Next Day

8 **The next day, remove the bowl from the fridge and scrape the dough out onto a floured board.**

9 **Massage or work the cold dough with your hands to loosen it up a bit and then begin to knead it until the dough is elastic and smooth, about 5 to 7 minutes. Allow to rest.**

Note: Kneading requires you to fold the dough over itself while pressing down with the heel of your hands and pushing it out away from you and bringing it back toward you with your fingers, thereby thoroughly combining all the ingredients and achieving an elastic, smooth dough. If the dough seems to stick to the board, sprinkle more flour onto the board.

10 **To prepare the muffin tins, do your *mise en place*** (see Tip 1) **for the steps below.**

11 **Grease each cup, sides and bottom, with a bit of softened butter.**

12 **Additionally, melt two sticks of butter in a small saucepan.**

13 **Add 1 teaspoon of the melted butter, 1 teaspoon brown sugar, 1 teaspoon of white corn syrup, and 1 teaspoon pecan chips to each cup.**

14 **Form the dough into a ball and cut it in half.**

For each half of the dough, follow the directions below:

15 **Roll the first half of the dough until it covers the board making a 9" by 12" rectangle (approximately.)**

16 **In a medium-sized mixing bowl, make a paste by creaming together 1 stick of softened butter with 1 tablespoon cinnamon and ½ cup brown sugar** (see Tip 2).

17 **Spread the paste evenly over the dough rectangle, covering the entire surface from edge to edge.** An offset spatula is very useful for this task.

18 **Starting from the 12" side, roll dough into a long snake, like a jellyroll.**

19 **Cut this roll into two parts.**

20 **Cut each part into 12 even slices, placing each slice into one muffin cup.**

21 **Repeat until 24 slices have been made and two muffin tins have been filled.**

Follow the directions with the second half of the dough from steps 15 to 21.

22 **Cover each filled muffin tin with a pristinely clean dishtowel and allow to rise in a non-drafty place for about 2 ½ hours.**

23 **When doubled in bulk, bake in a preheated 350 degree oven for 30 minutes or until golden brown.**

24 **Cover a board with tin foil, turn out each finished tin upside down by flipping the muffin tin so the rolls fall out onto the tin foil surface.**

25 **You may need to scrape out some of the topping that sticks to the bottom of each muffin cup and place it with a spoon on top of any roll that is bare of the melted pecan, brown sugar mixture.**

Serve warm with morning coffee or as a dessert with coffee and vanilla ice cream if you dare!

Note: These freeze beautifully. Store in a covered container or Ziploc freezer bag. Warm before serving.

Schnecken (or Sticky Buns) *continued*

TIPS

1. *Mise en place* is a French term used by chefs to refer to the preparation of all ingredients before beginning any recipe. Each ingredient is placed in its own prep bowl and assembled on a cutting board or suitable surface. As you follow the recipe directions, each ingredient has been measured and gathered in one place, making your cooking more accurate and more efficient. If you get in the habit of doing the *mise en place* each time you cook, you will see its advantage.
2. Creaming butter and brown sugar together requires mashing the stick of butter in a bowl with a wooden spoon until pliable and soft, adding the brown sugar and cinnamon and incorporating them into a spreadable paste.

THE CHICAGO HOT DOG:

An Interview With Doug Sohn

One of the great things about the Chicago hot dog is, when well done, it is visually stunning.

I mean, it has all these colors, it looks great, it looks incredibly appetizing especially if it has a little bit of the char marks, the BBQ grill marks. And you have the brown bun, you have this neon green relish, you have red tomatoes, you have white onions, and this bright yellow mustard. And so when you see it, it looks like you want to eat it.

– DOUG SOHN

The Chicago Hot Dog: An Interview with Doug Sohn

The Chicago Hot Dog! There is none better in the USA.

Instead of trying to figure out our own recipe for the Chicago hot dog, we went to the source, Doug Sohn, the founder and former owner of "Hot Doug's." Clearly from its 2001 opening until its 2014 closing, Hot Doug's was THE place to get the best tasting, most authentic Chicago-style hot dog.

The restaurant is legendary. In fact, when Doug announced he was going to close the restaurant in October 2014, the waiting line, already regularly long, now began forming and continuing around the block some 12 to 24 hours ahead of the doors opening. People wanted to eat those hot dogs.

Here is our interview with Doug (conducted on 1 September 2014), giving you his hot dog philosophy, his vision for a great Chicago-style hot dog, and some tips and cautions for embarking on this culinary adventure yourself, now that Hot Doug's doors are closed.

Doug Sohn: My feeling about hot dogs is the same as any food. It's the same as fresh fish, it's the same as a good steak, it's the same as the best sushi you're going to have. Whether it's foie gras, whether it's a lamb stew, it is the ingredients. It's starting with the best ingredients and not screwing it up, not overcooking it, not over or under seasoning things. But it really boils down to the best ingredients.

And right off the bat, the hot dog has to have the natural casing.

The natural casing, which is most often a lamb intestine, (yes, that is exactly what it is), or pork.

The casing provides what is usually called "the snap." And that provides not only texture, but a little bit of flavor as well. That kind of crunch, that kind of snap that it gives, is a real satisfying element to eating a hot dog.

And that's called a "natural casing?"

Doug Sohn: Yes, the natural casing. A lot of hot dogs are skinless. They are done with a plastic-like casing when they're smoked or cured and then that's later removed. So, a lot of hot dog stands in Chicago use those or they're in the grocery store. One, they're cheaper, as without the casing it is less labor. And two, they're more uniform. It's just easier to process without a casing, so you end up with a cheaper product, not bad, but less expensive.

Casings, you know, are a natural element. So it varies in size and shape. But for me there's just something missing when you don't have the natural casing.

After that, it is the actual meat used in the hot dog. I think this is incredibly subjective. Growing up in Chicago it's a beef city, classically beef, the hot dogs were beef.

At the restaurant (Hot Doug's) we use the Vienna beef hot dog. One, it's a great local family owned company. Two, I think it tastes the best. It's the right balance of meat, of salt, of fat, and they use brisket and they use good cuts of beef.

You know the old joke about what the difference is between using lips and backsides versus using meat. Historically hot dogs were just those cuts thrown in there with some fat and scraps.

A good hot dog uses the good cut of meat whether it's veal, or pork, or beef. You're not using the scraps, you're using the quality cut and with brisket especially, there's so much flavor in there. You've a lot of marbling, and a lot of the meat itself tends to be more flavorful.

And are the ones you have at the restaurant all brisket or partly brisket and partly other things?

Doug Sohn: They're all brisket. Yeah, there is fat added to it as well and seasonings, but it's largely brisket. And you mainly want to start with that product. But a lot of it is regional. A lot of places have a pork tradition so they use pork meat or veal or combinations of pork, veal, beef and so forth. I personally like the beef flavor. I think it is a little bolder and it is a meatier flavor.

And it has to have the right amount of salt, pepper, garlic and other seasonings. And this is subjective. I like a little more garlic, but that's just my palate.

So, the classic Chicago dog is all beef, natural casing, poppy seed bun, yellow mustard, this neon green, sweet relish, tomatoes, onions, a spear of dill pickle, celery salt, and the little Mexican spicy sport peppers are optional.

They're called sport peppers in Chicago. You really don't see them in many other places. They are thin, green, pickled peppers. They add a little sweetness, but spice as well. Personally, I don't like the peppers because their spicy flavor covers up too much of the other flavors. The peppers tip the great balance of the other ingredients.

So, again, before I opened the restaurant my research found you can make bad Chicago hot dogs and one of the main reasons is using lesser ingredients. You can easily get stale buns, you can get cheap mustard, you can get poor quality tomatoes, you can get lower quality relish, pickles. Had one recently, not long ago at a sporting event here in Chicago, it was a bad pickle, you can get bad pickles.

The hot dog is a composed sandwich, and if you have too much onion or not enough tomato, or too much of one of the elements it throws off the balance as it would any dish. If you are making a classic butter sauce, if you use too much of an ingredient like wine or salt or something, it's not going to taste as good. You strive for the balance.

We get fresh buns delivered every day, the classic Chicago hot dog is on a classic Chicago poppy seed hot dog bun and they are steamed. It adds a textural (element). The warmth of it, adds a textural element, a little bit of softness to it, without it being mushy. You don't want to over-steam it because then it gets watery. And it should be fresh, as fresh bread tastes better than stale bread. It is simple, yet a lot of hot dog stands I think don't care about that or really pay attention to that, and therefore, it's a stale bun, and it makes for a lesser product.

And so, we get a fresh delivery every day and we steam the buns properly to where they still hold together, but the bun still has texture and heft, but it's also not so dense. It's softened by the steam, and it's warm bread. It tastes awesome.

About how long do you steam them?

Doug Sohn: About five minutes or even less. If you just do one at a time it might vary.

You can microwave them, keeping them in the packet. Put them in the microwave, leave them in their box for about 40 seconds, and it's fine. It's the same process, it's steaming. (People sort of shy away from microwaves. No, microwaves do some things really, really well and steaming is one of them.) We go through the buns so fast, they don't sit, although they would probably hold for 5 to 10 minutes.

In cooking a hot dog there are many varieties. I have two favorites.

Steaming them in simmering water. Simmering sort of seizes the casing a little bit, so it gets it a little tighter and creates more of that classic snap. If you break it in half or bite into it, that's what it is...it's onomatopoetic. Do not use boiling water because that will make it too tough.

With all meats you should bring them to room temperature, out of the refrigerator, before you cook it. It's the same with hot dogs. Let them sit out for a little bit and let them come to room temperature. This will allow it to cook through, get hot without overcooking, outside to inside.

The other method I like is grilling. What I like about that is the sort of Maillard effect of the caramelization. You get that nice classic chargrilled, BBQ flavor. And you get a little bit of the crunch, a little bit of that smokiness added to it. You get a textural aspect of it as well, and that adds to the overall flavor of the hot dog.

Hot dogs are not quite foolproof although I have had badly cooked hot dogs. But they are very forgiving. You put it on the grill, at that point it's already cooked through. You can eat hot dogs raw, so what you are trying to do as a cook, is get it hot (you don't want to burn it), you want to get a nice char on it, and the casing starts to snap, break a little bit. So you get this nice textural element, and the juices kind of start running to the outside.

Like I said, it's a little more forgiving, so it's not like a piece of fresh turbot where it's like 30 seconds too long it's done. No, it's a hot dog. It'll also hold so you can move it to the cold part of the grill and it'll be ok for a stretch.

As mentioned above don't steam it too long or it gets tough and/or rubbery or the opposite, it gets mushy and you lose that nice textural aspect of it. So like any good piece of meat whether it's steak or a hamburger, you want to cook it properly to temperature. You don't want to undercook it, you don't want to overcook it.

One should use good mustard. I like yellow mustard with hot dogs; the elements of the vinegary-ness, and sharpness, and tanginess of the yellow mustard I just think matches up really nicely with the beefy aspect of the hot dog. It's another particular element.

I love all mustards; I love brown mustard, Dijon, but I just think yellow mustard goes particularly better with the hot dog. And you can buy bad yellow mustard. So use good yellow mustard, good quality. The one we use is Heinz, they make a really good mustard, and Plochman's (I am pretty sure it's still a local company). It's a classic, it looks like a barrel in the squeeze jar. Terrific yellow mustard. Both are like sharp, tangy, but well-balanced and it tastes like mustard, it's not watery, it's not off.

The neon green relish is a Chicago thing. Food coloring is added to this sweet relish. How that started I am sure was either by accident or some sort of marketing idea for it to stand out, but it gives it great color, too.

One of the great things about the Chicago hot dog is, when well done, it is visually stunning. I mean, it has all these colors, it looks great, it looks incredibly appetizing especially if it has a little bit of the char marks, the BBQ grill marks. And you have the brown bun, you have this neon green relish, you have red tomatoes, you have white onions, and this bright yellow mustard. And so when you see it, it looks like you want to eat it.

And the relish adds this sweet element too. So, with your Chicago hot dog, you have the sweet, you have the salty, you have umami, you have the sharpness, like the vinegar elements (this aspect is taken from the mustard), so the relish adds a little bit of crunch, a little bit of texture, but also this kind of nice sweet element.

Tomatoes are, again, another colorful item. But they also have a kind of vinegary-ness, and there is the texture of the tomato. Use fresh tomatoes. It's tougher in February. We generally use Roma tomatoes. I just think they have a little more flavor, a little more texture. I like the skin of them. They tend to just be more consistent throughout the year. (In summertime, if you have a good beefsteak tomato, yeah, use that or any other heirloom tomato which is really nice.)

We use a good dill pickle, not mushy, because it has that nice sour element too and texture. And it should crunch. It should be like a pickle you just want to eat on your own. And it should be the whole length of the spear, it should fill the dog, you should get a little bit of everything in every bite.

You cut it (longitudenly) in half and then in half again and maybe in half again. But you're keeping like the whole length of the pickle spear. You want the skin as well as the flesh of the pickle, so you get a little bit of that crunch from the pickle spear and that nice sour taste in every bite of the hot dog.

I personally prefer caramelized onions at the restaurant. I just like them more. I think you have crunchy elements already in there, from the pickle, from the tomato skin, a little bit from the relish. So you would get more of that kind of textural thing from the raw onion. I am just not as big a fan of raw onion. That's me personally.

We caramelize the onions slowly, in butter, a little salt and pepper, that's it.

Pan sauté?

Doug Sohn: Yeah, just let them sit, just let them sit and cook slowly for a couple of hours. We dice 'em up small, good amount of butter. In so doing, you're also adding butter to the hot dog, so you have this nice creamy, fatty element to it, which never hurts. I don't think I've ever uttered the words "too much butter." So for me, the caramelized onions give another sweet element to it but a different kind of sweetness from the relish. But having said that, a lot of people like raw onion. You have that flavor and it's great. And you still have those same elements. And added crunch from the onion, another textural item. And the sweet, oniony aspect of the onion adds to the hot dog flavor.

What is a good relish? Is the relish the same as a sweet relish turned green?

Doug Sohn: It's actually made with a food coloring, a neon green food coloring added to it.

Can you buy a good sweet relish?

Doug Sohn: Absolutely! Absolutely. Although you can make your own, it's one of those things like, "Why"? You can buy really good relish.

The celery salt we put on a Chicago hot dog adds salt, which is never a good thing. You already have saltiness in the hot dog, and it is really the only salty element at that point. So the celery salt adds a little bit more of that. And I think for me, when you do the Chicago hot dog, the celery salt should go on the top, should go on last. So the salt is really going on the tomatoes, the pickle, and a little bit of the relish.

The celery salt brings out more of those flavors, brings out more pickle flavor, brings out more onion flavor, brings out more tomato flavor, as salt does with food. So it's not just to taste salty. To me salt enhances, it really brings to the forefront the natural flavors in whatever ingredient you are salting. And again, it's another aspect of it.

Why celery salt is added probably is, like most invented things are, an accident. We use it at the restaurant.

One of the things I love about the Chicago hot dog is there are so many ingredients on it, that if you really don't like tomatoes, don't put them on there. There's enough other stuff going on, that even though you know it will be different, it will still be really good. I like the mix and matching aspect of it, whether you want the spicy peppers or not on it, whether you want raw onions or grilled, caramelized onions, we all have our own personal palates and biases.

It's the same for all kinds of food. Use the best raw ingredients you can. Cook them properly, paying attention, and composing the dish with care and detail.

And so you know, I ended up opening the restaurant because I had too many bad hot dogs. Not enough people were doing it properly, for a variety of reasons. When I opened the restaurant, the main reason was to do the best Chicago-style hot dog that I could do.

A Chicago hot dog is great when done well. It is a great sandwich.

SUMMARY

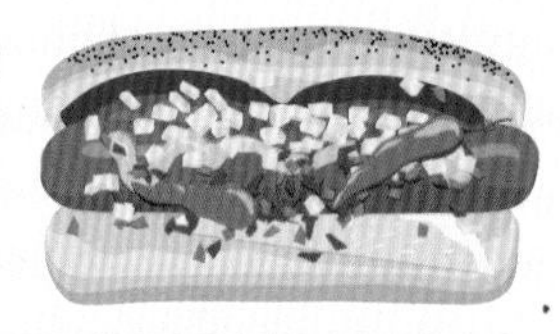

1. Hot Dog with natural casing. (We prefer all beef. Simmered in shallow water or charbroiled.)
2. Poppyseed bun. (Steamed for a few minutes.)
3. Yellow mustard (such as Heinz or Plochman's).
4. Tomatoes chopped. (Roma or Beefsteak or as desired.)
5. Onion (diced raw, or diced and slowly caramelized in butter.)
6. Sweet relish (bright neon green if available).
7. Pickle spears, longitudinally cut. (Get the highest quality available.)
8. Sport Peppers or peppers of choice if desired. (Use sparingly).
9. Celery salt (a mere dash added on top of the condiments).

LITTLE GEMS

If you are afraid of butter, use cream,

– JULIA CHILD

Little Gems and Leftovers

Little Gems and Leftovers came about because we often find ourselves preparing a quick meal, borrowing the basics from our main recipes, sometimes using leftovers from these recipes or just using whatever we find in our refrigerator and pantry. Although not as extensive as the original 45 recipes, these are delicious little gems. We thought they should be included and shared with you.

Many of these recipes give a second life to food, ways to turn a leftover into an unusual or delectable dish. As well, here you will find not-often-thought-of food combinations. Some are simple ideas to make your cooking more interesting or efficient.

We hope these thoughts will inspire you to give some "oomph" to a favorite food, a leftover dish, or to invent something totally new.

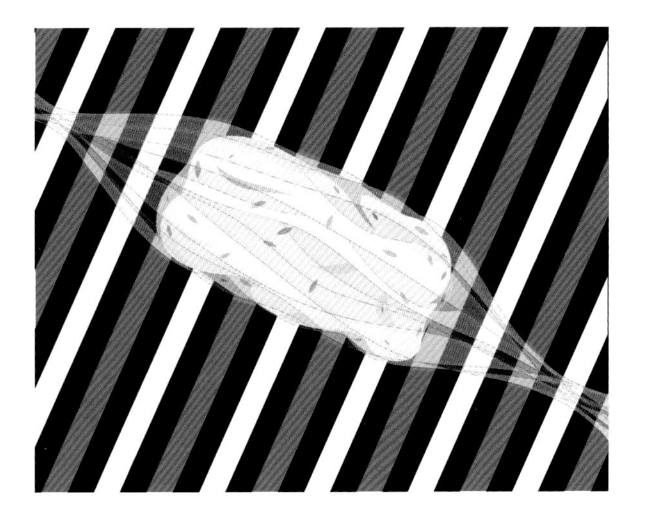

Butter

MAKES 8 TABLESPOONS

"If you are afraid of butter, use cream," Julia Child once said, but who is afraid of butter these days? Just use less if you have dietary restrictions. There is nothing quite like it for adding flavor to every food it touches.

Something we always have in our refrigerator is a compound butter. Compound butters are nothing more than butter enhanced with the flavors of herbs or spices, wine or even jam. Here are three versions that we highly recommend having on hand and they freeze beautifully.

1. Herbed butter

Soften unsalted butter in a medium sized bowl, creaming (see Tip 2, page 93) it to ensure that lumps are gone and a smooth butter paste results. Add to the bowl, a clove of minced garlic, a pinch of salt, 1 tablespoon of dried or minced fresh thyme or any herb you prefer. Rosemary and tarragon work well alone or in combination as does marjoram and oregano. Mix well to combine. Form into a log, wrap with parchment or plastic wrap, and refrigerate until firm and cold.

2. Mustard Butter

Begin as above with a stick of softened unsalted butter. Follow the steps for Herbed Butter, but instead of adding the herbs, add 1 tablespoon of Dijon mustard, 1 tablespoon of grainy mustard, such as Dijon's or Local Folks, 1 scant shake of cayenne pepper, 1 clove of minced garlic, and a pinch of salt. Proceed as with the herbed butter. Place the well-mixed butter on parchment paper or plastic wrap and roll into a log, wrapping the paper around the log and twisting the ends. Refrigerate until very firm.

3. Pepper Butter

As with the other compound butters, begin with a stick of unsalted butter, softened and creamed in a bowl. Add ¼ teaspoon of freshly ground black pepper, ¼ teaspoon of other ground pepper, such as red berry peppercorns or Szechuan peppercorns, 1 teaspoon of crushed fennel seeds, and a pinch of salt, and a small shake of cayenne pepper to taste. Mix well and place on parchment paper or waxed paper and form into a log. Proceed as with the other butters.

Cabbage Sauté

SERVES 2

For a really fast and delicious supper, just take a ½ head of cabbage, perhaps a leftover ½ head you did not use when making coleslaw, and coarsely cut it into bite-sized pieces.

Dice ½ of a medium yellow onion or a whole small one.

Melt a tablespoon of butter, add a splash of olive oil (so the butter does not burn) and add the onion and sauté until translucent. Add the cabbage, season with salt and plenty of freshly ground black pepper and sauté until slightly colored.

Nestle a veal bratwurst or two or a handful of fully cooked, tail-on-shrimp into the cabbage and continue to cook until sausage is well-browned and shrimp are cooked through. Voilà! Dinner in about 15 minutes.

Not new, but very tasty and quick.

Cauliflower Whip

SERVES 2

Is it cauliflower or is it mashed potatoes?

Cauliflower is a versatile veggie and this quick recipe is a terrific substitute for those who find mashed potatoes too heavy or too high in calories. Steam a whole cauliflower (or use any leftover cauliflower) cut into bite-sized pieces or florets.

When tender, place cauliflower in a Vitamix or other professional blender with 2 tablespoons of olive oil, a grating or two of fresh nutmeg, and salt and pepper. Vary the flavor by adding a ½ teaspoon of dried thyme, tarragon, oregano, or a pinch of lemon zest.

Blend until smooth and velvety or stop short of that if you prefer a rougher texture.

Serve immediately.

Cilantro Aïoli

MAKES ABOUT 1 CUP

As an alternative to our mock aïoli sauce (see recipe, page 72), try this for a quick and unusual sauce.

Take 1 cup of good mayonnaise (we use Hellman's), 1 teaspoon Dijon mustard, ½ bunch of cilantro, including some of the stems, washed and trimmed, the juice of ½ of a lime or to taste, ½ teaspoon of the zest of ½ of a lime, 1 large clove of garlic finely minced, salt and pepper.

Chop the cilantro very finely using a sharp chef's knife or a mini-Cuisinart chopper. Add the cilantro and all the remaining ingredients to the bowl and mix very thoroughly. Place in a jar and cover tightly and refrigerate for an hour before serving.

There is something about the lime and cilantro that when developed with the mayo and garlic is absolutely delicious and magically so.

Serve with cold shrimp, as a dipping sauce with French fries, with any cold meat or fish, or as a sandwich spread. Makes about a cup of sauce.

Cornbread

SERVES 4

This easy, quick to assemble corn bread is hands down the best we have ever tasted. This recipe is an adaptation from a too complicated recipe and which we believe should be preserved for all time it is so delicious. It is also a great way to use up leftover corn.

Preheat the oven to 350. Lightly oil a 9 or 10 inch cast iron skillet and put it in the oven to heat up.

Melt ¼ cup butter, set aside. Measure 2 cups corn (fresh or frozen) set aside.

Prepare all of the dry ingredients below in one bowl, mix together, and set aside:

2 cups all purpose flour, 1 cup yellow cornmeal, ¾ cup sugar, ½ teaspoon salt, 1 tablespoon baking powder.

Prepare all of the wet ingredients below in another bowl:

2 large eggs, 1 ½ cups whole milk,
1 ½ tablespoons vegetable oil.

Whisk the wet ingredients together thoroughly, add to the dry ingredients, add the corn and melted butter and combine until just mixed.

Pour into the hot cast iron skillet, knock the pan on your counter to distribute the batter evenly, and bake for about an hour or until the top is golden brown and a knife inserted in the middle comes out clean.

Cranberry Pear Relish

MAKES ABOUT 2 CUPS

Buy too many bags of cranberries for the holidays? Here is a cranberry relish that is perfect for anytime of the year and can be served with several different kinds of food. A sweet/tart relish, delicious accompanying rich fatty meats, such as pork ribs, braised or barbecued beef short ribs, duckling, or with roasted root vegetables. It brings memories of Lingonberry sauce, served at Scandinavian smorgasbords.

We also love it served with a cheese platter with several kinds of cheese, both hard and soft, crackers, good toast, nuts and pieces of dried fruit. Its sweet tanginess is a good contrast to the saltiness of the cheese.

This is easy and quick to do. A creation of Carol's son, Nick, it will take about 40 minutes to put together from beginning to end, though like many foods we love, it is even better the next day when all those flavors have married up.

Use a 3 to 4 quart saucepan, preferably a non-reactive, medium-sized enamel-lined pan, such as a Le Creuset. You will need a wooden spoon or paddle.

Take 1 cup water, ¾ cup sugar, a pinch of salt, 2 or 3 tablespoons grated fresh ginger (or to taste), ½ teaspoon cinnamon (or to taste), 1 bag of fresh or frozen cranberries, picked over for stems and bits, and 4 or 5 firm pears, peeled,cored, quartered, and cut into half inch pieces.

Place the first five ingredients into a medium sauté pan and bring to a boil, stirring until the sugar is dissolved.

Add the cranberries and pears and bring back to a boil.

Lower the heat and simmer uncovered until the berries pop and the mixture becomes jammy, about 15 to 20 minutes.

Allow it to cool to room temperature, as it will thicken and the flavors will develop.

Store in a glass jar, preferably overnight.

Fast and Delicious Strawberry Jam

MAKES ABOUT 2 CUPS

We love strawberry jam or *confiture*, as the French call it.

In August when strawberries are coming to the end of their summer season and tend to be very ripe, this is a great time to make a few jars of this ambrosia.

This quick recipe requires none of the boiling, fuss and bother that usually goes into the canning process and should you have over-purchased strawberries, your eyes being bigger than your stomach, take the opportunity to make jam. You will love it and it is ridiculously easy.

It is perfect on Pan-Fried Toast (see recipe, page 56), over ice cream, or serve it in a small pot on our Cheese Board (see recipe, page 113).

Take two pounds of strawberries, remove leaves, halve the berries if large, leave some small ones intact, and wash quickly in cool water.

Place in a large bowl and sprinkle with ½ cup of superfine sugar, and two teaspoons of vanilla extract. Mix well until berries are coated with sugar.

Heat the oven to 350 degrees.

In a rectangular baking dish (about 8" by 12") distribute the sugared berries evenly in the dish.

Bake for one hour to 90 minutes, stirring every 20 minutes or so. The cooking time will vary depending on the ripeness of the fruit and the accuracy of your oven. When cooked, squeeze the juice of a half of a small lemon or grate a teaspoon of orange rind into the jam and stir to combine.

Cool slightly and place in glass jam jars. When completely cool, seal with tight lids, and refrigerate.

This recipe works equally well with peaches or a combination of peaches, strawberries, and blueberries.

Do not worry about how long to keep it. It will not last!

Potato Cakes

ABOUT ½ CUP MASHED POTATOES PER POTATO CAKE

Potato cakes are an old family favorite. They are made with leftover mashed potatoes, shaped into a patty, dusted with flour, salt, pepper, and then fried in butter until crisp and golden on each side. The crunchiness of the outer crust as you bite into this potato cake along with the soft, creamy mashed potato under the crisp coat is a delectable combination. Be sure to have extra mashed potatoes for this purpose. The mashed potatoes (see recipe, page 50) you made have seasoned and developed flavor while waiting in the refrigerator. Turning out these delicious morsels is a treat all in themselves.

For those who may be confused about the difference between a potato cake and a potato pancake, simply put, a potato cake is made from leftover mashed potatoes while a potato pancake (aka, latke) is made from grated, raw potatoes (see recipe, page 54).

Take cold mashed potatoes out of the refrigerator and allow to come to room temperature for about 15 minutes. Spread some flour on a board and place each patty on it and turn to lightly coat each side with the flour. Form a handful of potato into a patty about the size of a small burger, and a good inch thick.

Sprinkle with salt and pepper to taste. Remember, refrigerated food loses its salt flavor.

Melt 2 to 3 tablespoons of butter in a mineral or cast iron skillet over a medium flame and when hot and foaming, place each patty in the skillet and cook until thoroughly brown on one side. This may take up to 10 minutes. Flip potato cakes, turn the flame down to low and cook until thoroughly brown and the edges are crispy on the other side.

These are divinely delicious. You will always want to make more mashed potatoes than you can eat at one meal, to assure you have plenty of leftovers for these potato cakes!

Potato Salad Redux or Hash Browns

SERVES 2

Should there be any of our leftover potato salad (see recipe, page 52), it makes really great hash browns. The already prepared potato salad has married flavors of potato, good mayonnaise, onion, and bacon. So, think about it, all the components of hash browns are present and accounted for!

Heat a skillet to medium to medium high, preferably cast iron or a mineral steel skillet to ensure a good browning, melt a little butter in it (about a tablespoon or so), add a little olive oil so the butter does not burn, and when the skillet is hot, add the leftover potato salad.

Take a spatula and press down gently from time to time on the potatoes to assure even browning. Leave them undisturbed for a good 5 to 10 minutes. With a large metal spatula, turn the potatoes and cook on the second side until golden brown and crisp. Serve immediately. Amazing!

Prunes as an Appetizer

SERVES 2 TO 3 PRUNES PER PERSON

Prunes are nothing to be afraid of, truly. Here is a delicious way to use them.

Take pitted prunes (the large French ones, St. Dalfour are very good) and make a small slit on one side. Remove the pit and stuff the hollow with a teaspoon or so of soft goat or blue cheese (We often use Bleu d'Auvergne). Squeeze the sides gently together and secure with a toothpick.

This is a great hors d'oeuvre or as an additional piece on a cheese board (see recipe, page 113).

Quick-to-Prepare Barbecued Chicken

SERVES 4

This succulent, tender chicken dish is very easy and quick to put together, even though it takes three hours to cook in the oven. We recommend it highly because of its deep flavor and the convenience of a one pot dish.

We especially like to make it when we have leftover BBQ sauce from our Baby Back Ribs—Chicago Style (see recipe, page 38) or our homemade barbecue sauce for the Braised Short Ribs (see recipe, page 70).

You will need the following tools,

A large Le Creuset skillet or other oven appropriate skillet or pan with a cover and a large mixing bowl.

The ingredients are pretty simple:

Olive oil

1 cut up whole chicken (8 pieces)

1 large bottle of Sweet Baby Ray's Barbecue Sauce

½ to 1 cup orange juice (preferably fresh)

1 medium yellow onion, sliced

5 to 6 garlic cloves, lightly mashed

½ cup white wine

Salt and pepper

In a large bowl, mix the barbecue sauce with the orange juice, set aside. If making in advance, refrigerate up to 48 hours.

Heat the skillet or pan over medium high heat with about ⅓ cup olive oil.

Add the chicken and brown on all sides. Turn the heat down to medium. Then remove the chicken from the skillet or pan and set aside.

Pour off all but 1 tablespoon of accumulated fat. Put back on the heat.

Add the onion and garlic and sauté until soft.

Deglaze the pan with the wine.

Add the chicken back into the skillet, sprinkle with salt and pepper.

Pour the barbecue sauce over chicken and vegetables.

Place the covered skillet in a 250 degree oven and cook for about three hours.

Best if made a day in advance to allow the flavors to marry.

Absolutely delicious.

Rethinking Brussels Sprouts

SERVES 2

Here is a vegetable that many find boring or too reminiscent of cabbage. If you can take an extra few minutes, cut the stem end off of a dozen or so individual Brussels spouts and then with your fingers, pull the leaves apart, separating them from the whole sprout.

You will easily fill a bowl with these leaves, all from a handful of Brussels sprouts!

If that is too much work, then slice the Brussels sprouts thinly into ribbons beginning at the narrowest end or non-root end.

Sauté the leaves or slices in two tablespoons of butter and a splash of olive oil (so the butter does not burn) with a clove of minced garlic, one tablespoon of minced fresh ginger, salt and pepper until crispy and caramelized. For variety, add a pinch or two of your favorite herb or a small sprinkling of celery seed or fennel seed.

Absolutely delicious and totally un-cabbage-like.

Roasted Tomatoes

MAKES ABOUT 2 CUPS

A great tomato sauce can be had by draining a can of San Marzano whole, peeled tomatoes, cut them in half and place them evenly on a sheet pan lined with parchment paper.

Evenly distribute the following on top of the tomatoes: a few sprigs of fresh thyme, and rosemary, a cut up onion or a shallot or two, as many garlic cloves as you would like, peeled or not, a half lemon if you have one left over, sprinkle with salt and pepper, a slight shake of red pepper flakes, and drizzle all of it with good olive oil.

Bake at 325 for 45 minutes to an hour. Discard the thyme and rosemary branches, scrape the rest into a bowl or sauce pan to keep warm.

Serve with pasta or forget the pasta and eat it by itself as the evening's veggie. It is also so delicious with scrambled eggs or mixed with cooked gigantic white beans (but then add some chopped fresh sage and a splash of white wine while the beans are warming with the roasted tomatoes).

They are equally delicious on our Pan-Fried Toast (see recipe, page 56), almost like a cooked bruschetta, with an extra drizzle of olive oil over it and a chiffonade of fresh basil (roll three leaves of fresh basil like a cigar and slice it into ribbons and spread evenly on top), and sprinkle a little sea salt as a finishing touch. And they will not taste like canned tomatoes, promise!

Spiced Olives

MAKES ABOUT 2 CUPS

This quick-to-fix hors d'oeuvre is equally good as a snack, cut up in salads, as an addition to pasta sauce, or as an additional topping on our Peewee Pizza (see recipe, page 16). As with almost every do-ahead recipe of ours, these benefit greatly from making them in advance, giving their flavors 24 hours to marry. The longer you keep them, the more intense the flavors.

Purchase any combination of green and black olives available to you. We prefer Kalamata, French Nicoise, French Lyon, Liguria, Gaeta, Picholine, or any unstuffed olive. We like the olive bars at grocery stores where the olives are loose, the variety is greatest, and you are permitted to purchase as few or as many as you want.

In a large bowl, place about 2 cups of olives, well-drained of their brine or oil if they come with any. Sprinkle the olives with fennel seeds to your taste, we use a good healthy tablespoon per 2 cups of olives. Mince 2 to 3 cloves of garlic (or to taste) and mix it into the olives, distributing it throughout. Add a shake of red pepper flakes to taste and mix well.

Place in glass jars and pour in enough good fruity extra virgin olive oil to nearly cover. Seal tightly with a secure lid. Best served after 24 hours. These will keep in the refrigerator for several weeks if they last that long. Before serving, allow to come to room temperature first.

The Best Sautéed Onions

SERVES 2

Here is a delicious way to do onions. Use them as a snack by themselves or add them to other dishes, such as the Chicago Hot Dog (see SUMMARY, page 104).

Take an onion, yellow, red, or white. Cut off both ends. Cut it in two and remove the outer paper. Slice it into not too thin moon-shaped slices by slicing each half from top to bottom.

Melt two or three tablespoons of unsalted butter in a cast iron skillet, mineral steel pan, or a stainless steel skillet preferably resting on a diffuser over medium heat. Add a tablespoon or two of olive oil, so the butter will not burn. The olive oil will balance the water content in the butter and prevent burning. Add the onions and distribute them evenly in the pan.

Turn the heat down and set the heat somewhere between low to medium depending on how much time you have. On low heat, cook for some 3 to 5 hours. On medium heat, cook from 45 minutes to 1 ½ hours. Stir occasionally.

Take them off the heat when they reach the desired doneness. We prefer them a deep golden bronze or darker.

The St. Louis Dessert

SERVES ABOUT 1 CUP BERRIES PER PERSON

Those who were born and raised in St. Louis, a city that has always had a special place in its heart for Chicago and a short trip away, know about this fruit dessert. Its origins remain a mystery, but its simplicity and deliciousness is undisputed.

Quite simply, take cleaned and picked-over fresh blueberries, place in individual serving bowls. Sprinkle generously with brown sugar and then a dollop of sour cream. That's it! Yum!

The First Or Last Bite

A simple cheese platter can be an elegant beginning or ending to a meal. For that matter, it can take the place of a whole meal!

Here are some ideas for putting together a delicious and beautiful cheese board. Best part other that eating it? It can all be done well in advance.

In composing a cheese board think of four or five varieties of cheese; hard and soft, sweet jams, and some savory items, too. Think of color, as the arrangement should be appealing and eye-catching, irresistibly drawing your guests to it.

SAVORIES

Goat cheese, Humboldt Fog or French Boucheron

French or Italian Blue Cheeses, such as a soft Gorgonzola

Deep yellow English Cheddar

Sliced sausages with garlic and fennel

Prosciutto or Mortadella, two Italian deli meats

SWEET ITEMS

Black Raspberry jam, (we prefer Stonewall Kitchens)

Fast and Delicious Strawberry Jam, (see recipe, page 109)

Clover Honey

Garlic and Onion Jam, (we prefer Stonewall Kitchens)

DELIGHTS THAT GIVE VARIETY AND SURPRISE

Prune Appetizer, (see recipe, page 110)

A Store Bought Pâté, perhaps one flecked with truffles

Spiced Olives, (see recipe, page 112)

Rainforest Crackers imbedded with dried fruits and nuts

Slices of a good baguette

Pan-Fried Toast (see recipe, page 56)

Salty nuts

Crisp Apple slices

Red and green grapes

Preserved fruits in Syrup

We know people who prefer this cheese platter with a glass of wine or a mug of beer and nothing more than a small piece of dark chocolate!

Techniques and Equipment

The purpose of this cookbook has been to bring you the best 45 recipes of their genre that we have collected, discovered, and developed over the years. In order for the recipes to be truly stellar it has required that we utilize some invaluable cooking techniques. We give them to you here, making your cooking preparation more polished, more complete, and in many cases easier.

Throughout the book, at the end of many recipes, we give tips we felt were more meaningful in the context of each recipe. Here you will find tips and techniques which apply more broadly.

Most cookbooks take for granted that the reader is already familiar with the techniques and equipment that will help achieve the most professional results. In our book we do not assume this, and we impart to the reader the tips and techniques we find most useful for creating the best recipes. Most of them are basics and will serve you well across the board. We suggest that you use our book as a resource, mining it for whatever recipes, techniques, and tips are most useful to you.

Diffusers

Although rarely used in the home, the diffuser is a vital tool in temperature control and distribution. It consists basically of a square or round piece of metal (we use a copper diffuser by Bella) that sits over one of the burners on the stovetop and evenly distributes the heat over the entire bottom of the pan and provides a buffer against direct flame and heat. Direct heat targets the center of a pan, much like a candle flame, causing hotspots (uneven cooking). With the use of a diffuser, the heat is spread out, allowing for a more even distribution of the heat. If you wish the same temperature applied to the pan as with direct heat, you must turn up the flame to compensate for the buffering quality of the diffuser.

We first used a copper diffuser in cooking eggs as we believe the more evenly the heat is distributed and the more gently applied, the better the egg. We also use the diffuser when simmering foods for hours such as reducing sauces, slow cooking onions, meat or fowl, because the diffuser allows slow, even cooking for hours. We even use a diffuser for popping corn at high heat as it not only distributes the heat evenly, it allows us to vigorously slide the pan back and forth over the smooth surface of the diffuser, keeping the kernels moving, redistributing them to the bottom of the pan where the hot oil is, and resulting in a pan of popped corn with no or very little hard tack (unpopped kernels).

Hand (Kitchen) Towels

Many home cooks use oven mitts to protect against hot pans. We do not, and neither do most professional cooks. We use hand or kitchen towels and they are an indispensible tool for the home cook as well.

We rarely see a professional cook use mitts (except in outdoor grilling) because they do not allow for a secure grip. A kitchen towel is much easier, safer, and more useful for other purposes as well. We keep several kitchen towels hanging on our oven door and others folded up next to the cooktop for ready use in picking up hot pots or to wrap around the handle of a hot pan just pulled from the oven as a "don't touch!" warning. We use them to rotate a roasting chicken, grabbing the bird with two towels, impeccably clean of course, to turn it and complete its roasting.

In many cases, these are towels that have seen their better day. While clean as can be, they may have permanent spots or burns on them and they will be discarded in the near future. Clean them in the laundry by themselves with hot water and detergent and they will be hygienic again, but do not expect all of those stains to come out. The towels are not pretty, but they work. Spills, dirty spots, and juices are all cleaned quickly with one of these towels and your hands are perfectly protected from hot pots and pans.

Paddles vs. Spoons

One of the most overused cooking utensils is the wooden spoon. We have found the paddle much more effective in almost all circumstances.

A spoon and a paddle are not the same tool. They each have their own use, but strangely, the paddle is universally underrated, yet far more useful. Wooden paddles are efficient at moving ingredients off the relatively flat bottom and square shaped sides of a pan. The curved shape of the spoon causes some of the food bits to remain undisturbed whereas the square shape of the paddle allows it to fit snugly into the crevice where the sides and bottom of a pan meet, thus scraping up those valuable bits that give the food so much flavor.

This first came to our attention when another cook recommended we stir our scrambled eggs with a wooden spoon, as opposed to the silicone paddle we use on our nonstick skillet. We found the spoon would not cleanly move the eggs out of the crevices of the pan, nor off the flat bottom of the skillet. Its curved shape was doomed to miss bits and pieces of egg. A wooden or silicone paddle on the other hand beautifully moved the eggs leaving no dry residue behind to ruin the consistency.

The spoon has its uses, such as stirring a large pot of soup or for tasting, but we find its ubiquitous use perplexing and recommend that our readers try a paddle for more efficient cooking. (We use wooden paddles available at this writing from Michael Ruhlman's website.)

The Cast Iron Pan

One of the most useful, and perhaps misunderstood, tools of the chef is the cast iron skillet. You can tell an experienced chef by how and for what purpose he or she employs iron in cooking.

Cast iron is ideal for cooking at high heat, often producing wonderful caramelizing on foods. Some even like cooking fried eggs in cast iron, giving them a crusty bottom and crusty edges.

Primarily we find that cast iron is unsurpassed in cooking steak, hamburger, lamb burger, lamb chops, potatoes, bacon, or any food to which you wish to impart an exterior crust, normally employing high heat. We even use a large round platter-like cast iron grill (Lodge, 14-inch Baking/ Pizza Pan) to cook and crisp our Peewee Pizzas as it is big, affording space for several tortillas. And the pan can double as a diffuser or warming platter.

To cook meat with cast iron, you must be willing to turn up the flame to its highest level and let the pan get scorching hot. We have met home cooks who just cannot bring themselves to turn the heat on high under an iron pan, let alone for 4 to 5 minutes before cooking a steak, hamburger, lamb chops, or lamb burger. It is just something the good cook must get past.

One of the primary barriers to the use of cast iron is the misconception that its care is difficult or troublesome. We have found it is probably the easiest cookware to clean and maintain. There are many methods available on the Internet, but the basics are: Do not wash in soapy water. If you must, rinse briefly with hot water and a stiff brush and never when it is hot, and dry immediately. We never put our cast iron under any water. If you insist on wetting it, dry carefully and then heat gently on the stove top to thoroughly dry. Then apply a thin coat of oil with a paper towel. Normally, we just wipe the cast iron out with a paper towel after it cools to warm or if still hot, we use tongs to grasp the towel. Then, we remove any stuck-on material with a little metal, chain mail (available in cookware stores or online) used to clean cast iron, or we use a plastic scraper if food is not severely baked on. Then we apply a thin coat of Grapeseed oil over the bottom and sides of the pan and wipe any excess off with a paper towel, leaving a slight sheen.

Every few months, we will heat the pan on the stove top for 3 to 5 minutes or more on high heat, turn the heat off, pour a thin layer of Grapeseed or peanut oil in the pan, spread it around evenly, and let the very hot pan absorb it. Yes, cast iron is porous! (Some prefer vegetable Crisco or coconut oil for seasoning.) When it cools to warm, we wipe out the oil leaving a thin film, or again if still hot, we use tongs to hold the paper towel. This is a short form of seasoning. A more thorough method is to preheat your oven to 450 degrees, then turn it off and place the dry pan in the oven for one hour. This expands the pores. Take it out and rest until cool enough to handle with a kitchen towel. Use a paper towel with tongs to spread Grapeseed oil or Crisco around the surface of the pan, handle and all. Wipe clean, making sure to remove all the liquid. Do not leave it too wet as too much oil will cause smoke and baked on globbing. Turn the oven up to 500 degrees and bake the skillet, upside down, for another hour. You can put a baking pan or tin foil under it in case you left it too wet and it drips. Turn off the oven and let it cool down. This thoroughly seasons the pan. However, we find we rarely need to do this with proper daily care.

Generally, if the cast iron is kept slightly oiled at all times, it will last forever. Individual recipes in this book will give further care specifics.

Note: Cast iron and mineral steel pans (see page 117) are not ideal for pan sauces, especially those with a high sugar content or a high tomato content.

Old Versus New Cast Iron

There is a distinct difference between the old cast iron cookware and the newer cast iron. The older cast iron is largely coveted for its smoother metal surface that eventually creates a nearly nonstick cooking surface. However, the older cast iron is generally thinner than the new cast iron and, although this allows the pan to heat up faster, beware, as too high a heat will buckle it. The pan then will not sit flat on a burner and the food will not evenly settle to cook in the bottom of the pan. The newer, thicker cast iron such as made by Lodge, can take very high heat without buckling or warping. Hence, each has its use. We use the older, thinner, cast iron where high heat is not required such as slow cooking onions, making Peewee Pizzas (when not using the Lodge 14-inch baking pan), Pan-Fried Toast, pancakes, and fried potatoes. We use the newer, thicker cast iron for very high heat applications such as cooking steaks, seared roast beef, hamburgers, lamb chops, and lamb burgers.

Note: Putting any pan on the stove top flame subjects it to hot spots which can buckle thinner cast iron as well as the mineral carbon steel pan discussed below, whereas the same heat applied inside the oven is much more even, creating less hot spots. You can lessen this effect on the stovetop either by using a diffuser, or warming the pan up slowly before hitting it with high heat.

The Mineral Carbon Steel Pan

The mineral carbon steel pan is one of our favorites, but it is hard to say exactly when we prefer it to the stainless steel pan, or the cast iron pan.

Let's start out with what we do not use it for: cooking at very high heat, especially on the stovetop. For that, we use thick, cast iron only. If you put a lightweight mineral pan under a high flame on the stove top, it can buckle, just like the old, thinner cast iron. However, there are some companies such as de Buyer making thicker carbon steel pans that will be less prone to buckling under high, stovetop heat.

We use the carbon steel pan whenever we wish to impart a lovely crust or caramelization: Pan-Fried Toast, cooking Peewee Pizzas, frying potatoes (at medium to medium high heat), slow cooking onions for hours (finally achieving a crisp exterior to them), pan frying vegetables, and sometimes fish, like salmon (as it gives the fish a wonderful crust, searing the skin side until very browned and flipping it to the other side to quickly sear and finish).

We even cook fried eggs in well-seasoned mineral pans at low heat with generous amounts of butter.

And finally, we often choose the mineral carbon steel pan over stainless steel just because it is much easier to clean up, requiring just a wipe out with a paper towel and a thin coat of oil as described earlier in reference to cast iron.

That explains our consistent use of carbon steel.

Note: Metal pans (carbon steel and cast iron) are reactive, so acidic foods, such as tomatoes, can reduce or strip the seasoning of the pan. If so, just re-season the pan, preferably in the oven (the heat is more even than stovetop), as discussed in the previous cast iron section. Or use stainless steel for cooking tomatoes.

The Nonstick Pan

Like any tool of a cook, nonstick equipment has a specific use. It is not a universal pan or pot for all occasions and its use must not eclipse the use of metal pans in the kitchen. Although there have been technological advances in its ability to take higher heat, a nonstick skillet is best used on low or medium heat and where its nonstick properties are a priority.

For instance, a nonstick pan is nearly perfect for eggs as the egg does not stick to the pan and when taken off the surface, its appearance is not marred by bits and pieces sticking to the pan as might be the case in a metal pan.

Delicate fish also lends itself to cooking in a nonstick pan as the fish does not pull apart when removed for serving. (But here again, the cook must consider the desired final result since we use carbon steel pans on fish when we want to achieve a nice sear on the exterior of the fish. If you hit the fish hard with well-heated carbon steel, coated in olive oil, the fish will not stick.)

We even use the nonstick skillet for such items such as creamed spinach, when combining and slowly heating the ingredients. They slide around easily and remain separated from the pan.

Do not use hard or sharp objects on a nonstick pan, nor harsh detergents. Clean with soap and water and a medium-hard brush. Treat your nonstick pan gently and it will last much longer.

The Stainless Steel Pan

Gorgeous to display in your kitchen, stainless steel is great all around cooking equipment. Using a skillet or a pot, you will achieve good results whether boiling water for steaming, using an insert to boil eggs, or sautéing mushrooms in butter in a skillet.

We use stainless steel for just about everything we use other metal skillets for, except very high heat situations. Stainless steel generally gives a more neutral flavor to foods than cast iron and carbon steel which add their own nuance of flavor due to a small buildup of food on them (seasoning). That is why you will want to thoroughly clean stainless steel after each use, removing any bits of burned-on food, ensuring a neutral cooking flavor.

This is the pan to use when making a pan sauce, utilizing the "fond" or browned bits left in the pan's bottom. (Scrape the bits up after hitting the hot pan with wine or other liquid, add other ingredients such as shallots, parsley, even cream, then reduce, and voila!) You can't beat stainless steel for making a pan sauce, especially one with a high sugar content, which tends to cling to cast iron and mineral steel after cooking, leaving a gooey mess.

Another advantage to stainless steel is that, unlike cast iron and carbon steel, acidic foods, such as tomatoes, do not adversely affect or interact with it. It works quite well for slow cooking tomato sauces, as does a Le Creuset pan.

However, stainless steel can often require a real scrubbing after use, especially if you have used butter, oil, or sugar. But it will clean up nicely by scrubbing with Barkeeper's Friend and something slightly rough, but nonscratch, such as a plastic Dobie sponge made by 3M, followed by warm, soapy water. (Always clean with soap after using a toxic detergent such as Barkeeper's Friend or Bon Ami to remove them completely.)

Le Creuset Cookware

These pots and pans fill a specialized and welcome niche in the kitchen. They distinguish themselves from other cookware by not only their stunning good looks, but also because of their gorgeous finish. Nothing beats them for long, slow cooking both on top of the stove or slow roasting in the oven. Because they are made of cast iron beneath their beautiful enamel coating, they retain and distribute heat beautifully.

Le Creuset is superb for long, low cooking of sauces as the ingredients do not react with the pan nor stick to it if proper temperature control is maintained. For instance, our Chicago Cream Sauce is slow-cooked in a shallow, wide Le Creuset saucier pan to utter perfection. We have found nothing better for this purpose.

And of course, we use it to slow cook meat, such as our Braised Short Ribs recipe. The result is tender and succulent.

For those who love tomato sauces, unlike cast iron or carbon steel, Le Creuset does not interact with the acid of tomatoes. (Stainless is also suitable for tomato sauces as it too is nonreactive, but we prefer Le Creuset for this purpose.)

What we never use Le Creuset for is high temperature stove top cooking which we reserve for other cookware such as cast iron or carbon steel. In fact, although Le Creuset cookware can take it, we never use it for high temperature oven cooking either.

As we do not obsess over leaving a perfect looking enamel finish (food stains after all), we simply clean Le Creuset pans by soaking them, sometimes overnight, in soapy water, and then cleaning them with a scratch-free rough sponge such as the Dobie sponge made by 3M to remove any and all food particles. This leaves them sparkling clean and any slight discolorations left are part of the charm.

A good cook uses the right pan for the right job.

Temperature Tips

Knowledge of temperature is vital to exacting results in the kitchen.

The first and most obvious aspect of temperature control is knowing the amount of heat to apply to a particular food, pan and cooking method. How many times have you seen cooking shows where the contestant overcooks or undercooks to a poor or unsatisfying result. This is learned through experience. For instance, it was only recently that we learned that cooking sliced onions for hours over very low heat (using a diffuser and iron pan) produces a wonderful flavor not achieved through the application of a higher heat normally associated with pan-grilled onions. The same could be said of our scrambled egg recipe. We found using very low heat for scrambling eggs over a low flame or a pot of steaming water produced the best result.

It took us much experimenting to figure out that certain meats tasted divine cooked at very, very high heat in a thick cast iron pan.

There is much more to temperature than the above. There is the subject of temperature distribution. Whether on the stove or in the oven we try to turn the pot or skillet 180 degrees every so often after the food has been cooking to ensure even heat distribution. Stove tops and ovens (less so) have hot spots and consistent turning alleviates this to a great degree. We often use a diffuser to distribute the oven top heat even more, especially when cooking at low temperatures for a longer period of time.

There is one aspect of temperature control of which many cooks are not aware and that is the sudden application of heat or cold. Too many cooks will take a hot pan and hit it with cold water. That will damage it. Never shock a pan with extreme changes of temperature. Let the pan rest and cool before subjecting it to cold temperatures.

In fact, you can buckle a metal pan when it is at room temperature by hitting it with high heat. This is why we often start our skillets or pans on low heat, gradually warming them up, and only then do we apply high heat to them before cooking.

Finally, there is the concept of the inertia of heat or cold. Carry over cooking is an example. You can take a pan off the heat, but it will still retain its temperature, only slowly cooling. Hence, when cooking eggs, steak or whatever, you need to remove the food from the pan before it is fully cooked as it will continue to cook off the stove or out of the oven. Or if you are shooting for a specific temperature, remember to shoot for five degrees shy of that figure as the meat, fish, or fowl will continue to cook after removal from the heat and sitting idle before serving.

Once you get the concept of how temperature affects your cooking and equipment, it will become second nature to getting great results.

Allowing Food to Marry

The term "marry" in cooking refers to the practice of combining foods either cooked or uncooked and allowing them to sit undisturbed for hours or for days. Allowing flavors to meld or marry can and does make a huge difference in the final result in many recipes and is one of the most underrated techniques. We have found this applies to such recipes as applesauce, soups, chocolate mousse, sauces, coleslaw, egg salad, BBQ Ribs, just to name a few.

Key to this is planning ahead so you leave time for the marrying. Although this might appear an inconvenience it actually is quite the opposite as the ingredients will be ready to serve at once without further preparation or ready to serve once heated up. Either way preparation is minimal, saving time and stress in coordinating the completion of a meal.

For that very reason, in this book we give you a heads up when marrying is required.

Many cooks underestimate this invaluable culinary technique. Do not be one of them.

Bread Freshness

Keeping bread fresh is not easy. Ideally, we buy freshly baked bread (or make it) and consume it that day or at the latest the next day, before the bread starts losing that fresh taste. But eating a whole loaf of bread at one sitting is uncommon. A partial solution is to freeze the bread immediately. We often buy a whole loaf of bread (such as artisanal breads) slice it and zip lock the pieces for the freezer, removing only as many slices as we need for grilled cheese or toast or whatever. It tastes quite good and we are never caught without bread.

We also use a "live bread", called Ezekial Low Sodium bread, made with living grain and no flour. It is so fresh and "live" that it needs to be frozen to keep the grain alive. When needed, we pull a piece or two from the freezer and use it for Pan-Fried Toast, grilled cheese, Egg-In-The-Bowl, to name a few, and find it a wonderful and healthy alternative to white bread.

Mise En Place

Mise en place is French for "putting in place" or "everything in its place." In the culinary world, it designates the preparation and pre-measurement of ingredients (chopped vegetables, spices, liquids, eggs, and other components) required or recommended before you actually put a meal together. *Mise en place* pre-organizes and pre-measures all ingredients so you have everything at hand (often in small individual bowls) before cooking or preparation begins. *Mise en place* ensures that you neither forget items essential to the recipe nor are you hampered by having to crack eggs, measure flour, and so forth while in the midst of cooking and preparing the meal. Its use is one of the signs of a truly professional chef and makes your cooking preparation infinitely more efficient.

Care of Wood In The Kitchen

We see so many cooks who are unaware of how to care for their wooden utensils and cutting boards. Worse, we have seen some soak their wooden spoons in water or heaven forbid, put them in the dishwasher. If wood is not properly cared for, it will dry out and crack.

Wooden utensils should be cleaned by briefly running under water, soaping them up, rinsing and then drying immediately. For cutting boards we spray them with white vinegar to help kill germs and clean off any food particles. From time to time we wipe both wooden utensils and cutting boards with food grade mineral oil to keep them from drying out. We let them sit overnight absorbing the oil. After doing this consistently, you will notice the wood is a richer color and less dry to the touch. This keeps the wood rich and moist.

BIBLIOGRAPHY

Beard, James. *Beard on Food: the best recipes and kitchen wisdom.* New York: Bloomsbury, 1974.

Beard, James. *American Cookery.* Boston: Little Brown & Co, 1972.

Child, Julia, Louisette Bertholle, Simone Beck. *Mastering the Art of French Cooking.* New York: Alfred A. Knopf, 1961.

Claiborne, Craig. *The New York Times Cook Book,* New York: Harper and Row Publishers, 1961.

Food Timeline: food history research service, www.foodtimeline.org.

Pollan, Michael. *The Omnivore's Dilemma: A Natural History of Four Meals.* New York: Penguin Books, 2006.

Rothman, Julia. *Food Anatomy: The Curious Parts & Pieces of Our Edible World.* North Adams, MA: Storey Publishing, 2016.

Ruhlman, Michael. *Ruhlman's Twenty: 20 Techniques, 100 Recipes, A Cook's Manifesto.* San Francisco: Chronicle Books, 2011.

Sitwell, William. *A History of Food in 100 Recipes.* New York: Little, Brown and Company,2013.

Tannahill, Reay. *Food History.* New York: Three Rivers Press, 1973.